KATHERINE JOHNSON

A LIFE STORY

Leila Rasheed

Illustrated by **Sarah Papworth**

■SCHOLASTIC

For Magnus.

First published in the UK by Scholastic Children's Books, 2019
Euston House, 24 Eversholt Street, London, NW1 1DB

A division of Scholastic Limited
London – New York – Toronto – Sydney - Auckland
Mexico City – New Delhi – Hong Kong

Text © Leila Rasheed, 2019
Illustrations by Sarah Papworth

ISBN 978 1407 19317 5

A CIP catalogue record for this book is available from the British Library.

Printed and bound by CPI Group (UK) Ltd, Croydon, CR0 4YY

Papers used by Scholastic Children's Books are made from wood grown in
sustainable forests.

1 3 5 7 9 10 8 6 4 2

www.scholastic.co.uk

CONTENTS

THE WATCHERS

The Eagle Has Landed

You could watch by standing outside at night and staring up at the Moon's blotchy disc in the sky – so familiar and yet suddenly so fascinating. You could watch from the comfort of your living room, if your family had a TV. In Britain, more likely than not, you all crowded into the living room of the one family on your street that was lucky enough to own a television set. Even if you couldn't watch, you could listen to the live broadcast on the radio. One way or another, the whole world was paying attention. The event that was being broadcast, live, was a "first" in human history – perhaps the most astonishing first ever.

More than 384,000 kilometres (238,000 miles) above the heads of every other living being, two men in a metal capsule were travelling at over 609 metres (2,000 ft) per second. They were about to try to do something no one else had ever achieved. They were trying to land on the Moon.

The capsule they were travelling in was called *Eagle*. It had been launched into space over four days before, on a rocket called *Saturn V* that took off from Florida, USA. The two men in *Eagle* – astronauts Buzz Aldrin and Neil Armstrong – had spent more than four days hurtling through lifeless, airless outer space to get to the Moon. They, along with a third astronaut, Michael Collins, who remained behind on the command module, had slept, eaten and gone to the toilet in a tiny, cramped metal box. If they managed to land on the Moon, it would still take them four days to get back. There was plenty of opportunity for the mission to go terribly wrong.

If it did go wrong – as other missions had gone wrong in the past – the 530 million watchers would not be seeing the most astonishing first ever, but a tragedy. If the mission failed, not only would it be a crushing disappointment for the USA, but also for anyone who had ever dreamed of a future beyond Earth. Manned missions to the Moon took money: 25.4 billion dollars (actual cost at the time), to be exact. They also took time. The goal of a lunar landing had been announced ten years earlier – for a decade, the government had poured huge amounts of money and resources into this near-impossible project. If this mission went wrong, spectacularly and on live television, it would be disastrous.

If it went right, it would be the first time that any human being had set foot on ground that wasn't part of planet Earth. If it went right, it meant almost anything was possible. It meant that Earth was not the end for humanity, but the beginning.

The Watchers

Throughout history, humans have looked to the sky for answers. Early civilizations followed the "movements of the stars" – of course, it was actually Earth that was moving! From their observations of the stars' different positions, they found out about time and the seasons. By watching the stars, whose apparent movements were regular and predictable from year to year, they discovered when to plant seeds so their crops didn't fail. Some of their observations only ended in more mystery – they marvelled at an eclipse or comet and wondered what it foretold.

One way or another, for millennia, humans have looked at the night sky to see the future. Now, they were seeing their future in the night sky again, but this time it was different. Mystery after mystery had been explained, understood and led to new discoveries and knowledge. Advances in science and technology had put men – and one woman – into outer space before, but for the first time, with the flight of *Apollo 11*, humans were going to set foot on an alien world … if it all went right.

The lunar module, steered by Neil Armstrong to a safe landing place, touched down gently on the Moon's surface.

A few moments later Neil Armstrong announced,

"THE EAGLE HAS LANDED."

530 million people breathed a sigh of relief.

The live broadcast continued, in flickering black and white. The sound was crackly and there were long silences as the astronauts prepared for descent. Finally, Neil Armstrong, in a bulky spacesuit, appeared at the door and climbed awkwardly down the ladder, the weak gravity of the Moon making it look a little as if he was climbing into a swimming pool. His foot touched the Moon, and his next words went down in history:

"THAT'S ONE SMALL STEP FOR (A) MAN, ONE GIANT LEAP FOR MANKIND."

Did Neil Armstrong say the word "a", or did he stumble over his lines and turn the first words spoken on the Moon into nonsense? There would be decades of argument and research to follow. But right then, it hardly mattered. In a single moment, Neil Armstrong and his companions had become the public faces of space. The date was 20 July 1969, and there were men on the Moon for the first time ever.

THE FIRST MOON LANDING

- Twenty per cent of the world's population watched the live broadcast of the Moon landing. It was the biggest audience for a live broadcast ever at that time.

- Do you know anyone who watched the event live? Why not ask your parents or grandparents if they saw it?

- You can watch the Moon landing here: **nasa.gov/multimedia/hd/apollo11_hdpage.html**

"Why Do We Need Women in Space?"

· ·

In 1969, it was never going to be a woman's small step on the Moon. In 1969 in the USA, women were expected to come second to men in everything, and to like it that way. White men ran everything – they ran the companies, made the laws and had all the power. It wasn't that women didn't want to become astronauts. In the 1960s, some women had gone through some of the same tests and challenges that the three men on the Moon had done as they trained to be astronauts, and in some cases the women had performed even better than the men. But even though the funding for their training was privately raised, and they passionately wanted to have a chance to try out as astronauts, NASA refused to allow the project to continue.

"Let's stop this now!" Vice President Lyndon Johnson scribbled across a memo about the Mercury 13, as they became known. No reason was given, probably because, to most people at the time, it was obvious: women's place wasn't in space.

WHAT IS NASA?

NASA stands for the National Aeronautics and Space Administration. Formed in 1958, it is the part of the US government that handles science related to flight on Earth and into space. Scientists, technologists and mathematicians at NASA do a wide range of work, including building satellites and training astronauts.

In a television interview with Jerrie Cobb, one of the women who had been part of the programme, the reporter asked a question that summed up the attitude of many at the time: "Why do we need women in space?" Cobb replied, "Why do we need men in space? It should be the best person..." Her logic did no good. The Soviet Union had already sent the first woman, Valentina Tereshkova, into space in 1963. The first American woman, Sally Ride, would not reach space until 1983, twenty years later.

Women in 1960s USA

Women were usually expected to be homemakers and housewives and their jobs were often seen as less important than men's. As a result, women had to fight for their rights at work, and for their financial independence. In 1969, the same year that men landed on the Moon, a woman called Lorena Weeks finally won a three-year court battle against the company she worked for, Southern Bell. When she had applied for a better role within the company, she had been rejected on the basis that "the man is the breadwinner in the family, and women just do not need this type of job". Weeks won her case, and Southern Bell were found guilty of discrimination, but the company's sexist attitude was widespread. Meanwhile, women had to fight for their right to work equal jobs for equal pay, and women of colour had an even tougher battle on their hands.

WOMEN WANTED TO BE ASTRONAUTS

"Being an astronaut at that time was the pinnacle of what you could do. You know, the whole world was watching. And when you step out on to the Moon there wasn't a person on the planet that didn't want to see you and didn't know who you were. And I think if that person was a woman it would have would have changed things. It would have seemed normal for women to do anything."

Heather Walsh, director of the documentary 'Mercury 13', quoted in the Guardian Online.

A Segregated Moon

Hard as it was for women to get into space in 1969, it was equally unimaginable that the USA would let a black man, rather than a white man, step on to the Moon first.

In the first half of the twentieth century it wasn't just the television broadcasts that were in black and white. It was the bathrooms, the hotels, the buses, the schools and the cinemas. Slavery had been abolished in 1865, but black Americans were a long way from being treated as equals: they were kept in poverty and exploited. In some states, the law said that they had to be segregated – not allowed to mix with white people and expected to see themselves as inferior to whites. They were not allowed to eat with, go to school with, or even use the same toilet as white people.

After black Americans had gained freedom, many hoped to be accepted as equal citizens alongside white Americans. Instead, white lawmakers and politicians quickly created racist laws and systems, to restrict what black Americans could do and where they could go. Even when the laws said they should be treated as equal, black Americans were often violently forced out of neighbourhoods, hotels and shops. White people who broke these racist laws – for example, the law against marrying someone who didn't share your skin colour – could be punished too.

This terrorising of black Americans by their fellow Americans affected the whole society, and the space programme was no exception. Many black Americans found it hard to be enthusiastic about space travel. What good was going to the Moon if they would only face racism up there as well as on Earth?

Fighting for Change

But in 1969, the year men landed on the Moon, change was coming on planet Earth too, though it had to be fought for every step of the way. Only the year before, in 1968, Martin Luther King Jr, a world-famous preacher whose powerful speeches demanded an end to oppression, had been shot dead. In 1969, the USA had the imagination to see that a man could set foot on the Moon, but not the imagination to see that black and white people could live equally together.

It was hardly surprising that black American men who aspired to be astronauts were driven out of training by racism. Ed Dwight was selected by President Kennedy to train as the country's first black astronaut, but left in 1966, saying he was driven out by racial politics. Another black astronaut, Robert Henry Lawrence, was tragically killed in an air accident before ever being sent into space. And though black American women dreamed of going into space too, a fortress of prejudice, against women and against black Americans, kept them from becoming astronauts for a very long time. Every woman who had the opportunity to try out as part of the Mercury 13 was white. The first black American woman, Mae Jemison, would not reach space until 1992 – nearly ten years after Sally Ride, the first white American woman.

And yet, some of the people who made it possible for Neil Armstrong to set foot on the Moon were not only women, but black American women to boot. These women had been employed for decades as mathematicians, unknown to most of the people who would be watching the Moon landing. NASA's achievements were built on the brains, courage and endurance of these women. One of them would become especially well respected for her work in space research. She was called Katherine Johnson.

Mary Jackson.

Katherine Johnson.

Dorothy Vaughan.

Christine Darden.

On 20 July 1969, Katherine Johnson was an adult with grown-up children, who had already lived through personal tragedy when her first husband died young. She was a brilliant mathematician who had survived a political system that tried to make sure she failed at school, and gone on to secure a job doing what she loved – mathematics at NASA.

NASA's laboratories, at Langley in the state of Virginia, were where the *Apollo 11* mission had begun. It was there that the astonishing human first – men on the Moon – had been made possible by intelligent people like Katherine working hard and thinking creatively. Without the scientists, engineers and mathematicians at NASA propelling them through the vacuum of space, Neil Armstrong and his crew would never have reached the Moon. When the world watched on television, hardly anyone would have realized that the astronauts bouncing around on the Moon, like lambs finding their feet, were part of a much bigger team. Most of those watching could not have imagined the huge amount of background work that had gone into the *Apollo 11* mission. There were so many things that needed to be taken into account, from the swiftly spinning, tilting Earth, to the fast-moving Moon. From launching the rocket safely, to landing the astronauts at a pre-determined spot to bringing them back again for a safe splashdown on Earth, every step in the mission had to be planned far in advance by people who stayed on Earth.

FEDERAL AND STATE

In the USA, 'federal' refers to organizations and laws that are passed by the national government in Washington, DC. However, each state has its own government and can pass its own laws. These can be different to federal laws and sometimes created to work against them. For example, when federal law gave black Americans the right to vote, some states passed new laws saying that only literate people could vote, knowing that many black Americans had never had the chance to learn to read or write.

But Katherine Johnson, who was watching the Moon landing on a television at *The Hillside Inn* in the Pocono Mountains in Pennsylvania, knew all about the background work. She had been part of the team that had done it.

Watching, she could feel proud that her brain had helped calculate how to pick up the astronauts and toss them on to another planet without breaking them. She had helped make America's greatest triumph possible. Without Katherine's calculations, America's flag would not have been the first to fly beyond Earth. Without her brilliant brain, the Eagle would never have landed, Earth's horizons would not have broadened and people's dreams of living on other worlds would not suddenly have taken on a new reality. For a black American woman who grew up in a segregated society and experienced prejudice throughout her lifetime, her achievement was even more extraordinary.

In later television broadcasts, Katherine Johnson has a powerful personality. She is a soft-spoken, elegant woman with an aura of calm confidence and a dry sense of humour. It is impossible to imagine her, back in 1969, making a big performance of her satisfaction that the Moon landing had been successful. However, she would have known perfectly well that those men would not have got to the Moon without her help.

Later on, President Nixon spoke to the astronauts on the surface of the Moon, in what he called "the most historic telephone call ever made". He told them: "Because of what you have done, the heavens have become a part of man's world." He was right. But they were part of "man's world" because of a woman's intelligence and hard work.

So, as Katherine watched, she felt glad and proud – but she also knew it was just part of her daily work. And that they still had to get the astronauts back again.

Reach for the Stars

Getting a man – or three – into space was only half the battle. Getting them back safely was crucial. If the first men on the Moon frizzled up on re-entry into Earth's atmosphere or were drowned when their module crashed into the wrong part of the sea, the rescue ship unable to get to them in time, then the whole mission would be seen as a failure.

Katherine had done the mathematical calculations that would launch the astronauts up to the Moon, but she had also done the ones that would bring them back to Earth safely, splashing down close to a ship ready to rescue them. In many ways this was one of the most nerve-wracking parts of the whole programme. The men had done their part, and the engineering had held up. To let them down at the last minute would be unbearable. But Katherine's brain was not in the habit of letting her, or anyone else, down.

At 12:51 pm on 24 July, the crew of *Apollo 11* splashed down just off the coast of the USA – in exactly the right position for the USS *Hornet* to cruise in and pick them up. The mission had been a complete success. Men had walked on the Moon and Earth had seen a vision of the future. Katherine's mind had tamed, explained and ordered the physical forces of the universe into manageable mathematics, to bring the capsule back down to Earth safely and get the men to their victory parade. The way Katherine saw it was the same way she saw all her successes: "It was my job, and I did my job correctly and well." However, it would be a long time before Katherine received her due recognition for the essential part she played in the USA's space victories.

"We can reach for the stars just as you have reached so far for the stars," President Nixon said as he welcomed the astronauts home. They were fine words, but Katherine Johnson did not need to be given permission to reach for the stars. Reaching for the stars was just how she, and many, many other black American women, had always lived their lives – refusing to accept the limits that others tried to force on to them.

MOON FACTS

- We only ever see one side of the Moon from Earth.
- The Moon is round, like Earth. We see it as a half or crescent because the Earth's shadow is blocking it from the Sun's light.
- The phases of the Moon guide farmers to know when to plant and harvest.
- The first calendars were lunar (based on the monthly cycle of the Moon, not the Sun). Some

important calendars in use today, such as the Islamic calendar, are lunar.

- The Moon is not always the same distance from Earth.

- The Moon was once a part of Earth. It is thought to have formed billions of years ago after Earth collided with another planet-sized body. The debris eventually formed into the Moon.

- The Moon's gravity causes the tides. As the Moon approaches Earth, water is pulled towards it, changing the sea level.

- The Moon doesn't shine with its own light, it reflects the Sun's light like a big mirror.

AS GOOD AS, BUT NO BETTER THAN, ANYONE ELSE

The Girl Who Asked Questions

Katherine Johnson was born Katherine Coleman, in a town called White Sulphur Springs, West Virginia. Way up in mountain country towards the east of the USA, it was a fashionable holiday destination that was popular with high society. Wealthy people came from the neighbouring state of Virginia, which was near the sea and had a more humid climate, to enjoy the cooler mountain air during the hot season. People had been coming to bathe in the natural spring water since at least the nineteenth century, believing it was good for their health.

Katherine was born on 26 August 1918, just as World War I was coming to an end. The USA had been involved in the war and servicemen from White Sulphur Springs had died in combat

Katherine herself, though, was not much affected by the distant war in Europe that had killed so many people. Though no one could have guessed it at the time, the consequences of that faraway foreign war would shape Katherine's whole life. World War I eventually led to rivalry between the Soviet Union and the USA, and to the so-called "Space Race". That competition between two of the world's most powerful nations, to control and conquer space, would provide Katherine with a career in the middle of the twentieth century, and – much later – with worldwide fame and respect for her achievements.

Katherine's childhood photos show a girl with bright, intelligent eyes and a big smile. Her family history was typical of the complex and often painful history of the USA. Her mother's grandfather had been a slaveowner, and he had owned her mother's grandmother. They had had four children. He had sent the children to school and to college. One of their daughters became Katherine's grandmother and lived on the same street as her. "We would go down and tell her we were hungry," Katherine once said. "Because she made such gorgeous pancakes!"

On the other side of her family, she had a Native American grandfather. Later in life, when interviewed, she said that her parents had never spoken about that part of their lineage. "They did not talk about it, not a word, until we began asking questions, lots of questions." Asking questions was one of Katherine's great strengths. She didn't simply have a gift for solving equations. She was determined, ambitious and she always wanted to know why.

THE TRANSATLANTIC SLAVE TRADE

Europeans invaded and colonized the American continent in the late 1400s. They began to farm crops like cotton and sugar, but they needed a large workforce. European slave traders kidnapped and enslaved African people, including children, loaded them on to ships and took them to the Americas where they were forced to work in horrific conditions. Many did not survive the journey. Those who did were condemned to a life as slaves, and their children were also enslaved. Slavery was made illegal in 1865. Many historians believe that the last person to survive the slave ships' journey across the Atlantic died in Alabama as late as 1937 – she is thought to have been kidnapped at age 12, and, tragically, never saw her parents or family again.

Working Backwards

Katherine had a very happy childhood. She had three siblings and loving parents. They were also parents who believed in the power of education and Katherine's own power to succeed. Her mother, Joylette, was a teacher. Katherine described her as a "born teacher: she was good at it". Katherine's father, Joshua, owned a farm where he bred horses, logged lumber and had an orchard. The farm did not pay nearly enough for the whole family to live on, especially in the years of the Great Depression.

THE GREAT DEPRESSION

Katherine grew up in a terrible time for most Americans. In 1929 the banking system collapsed, leaving many people penniless and everyone struggling to pay their bills and earn enough money to live on. This period was called the Great Depression. It also affected Europe, including the United Kingdom.

To earn more money, Joshua also worked as a janitor at the Greenbrier Hotel, an imposing building where many politicians and wealthy people stayed. The state would not educate black children past the sixth grade, so Joshua had to leave school when he was just eleven. Still, he was an intelligent man with a talent for mathematics and calculating complex sums in his head – Katherine said that he could look at a tree and know exactly how much lumber he would get out of it. In the same way, much later on in her career, Katherine would be able to "work backwards", calculating from where NASA wanted their astronaut to land and when, and tell them exactly what time a spacecraft should launch based on that information.

Katherine loved and admired both her parents, but "was definitely a daddy's girl". Her father always told her that she was "as good as anyone else – but no better". That saying would become the touchstone of Katherine's life: she would never fail to respect to others, and equally, she was never afraid to claim the respect that was due to her. As a child, when her white friends' fathers called her father by his first name, rather than the more respectful title and surname they used for white men, she responded by calling them by their first names, too. Throughout her life, Katherine was determined to step around the obstacles that racism tried to put in her way. "As good as anyone else" meant anyone – white people, too. But in the days of segregation, stepping around the obstacles could become a complicated dance. And if you put a foot wrong, it could be deadly.

"I Counted Everything"

Of course, in some ways, Katherine was better than others. She was significantly better at maths than most people, for example.

Right from the start, Katherine just loved numbers. "I counted everything," she said. "I counted the steps to the road, the steps up to church, the number of dishes and silverware I washed … anything that could be counted, I did."

She was working several grades, or years, above her age at school, skipping ahead of her older brother. Katherine even helped all her older siblings with their homework. Her parents could see she was intelligent. They wanted her to fulfil her potential and benefit from the best education she could get. But getting that education was not as easy as it should have been.

IT TOOK A WAR TO END SLAVERY

Slavery was made illegal in 1865, but it was not as simple as it sounds. Some states in the USA wanted to keep on owning slaves, so there was a civil war. The states that wanted to end slavery were called the Union, and the states that did not were called the Confederacy. The Union won and slavery was abolished. Many people in the Confederate states were not happy about losing the war and their slaves, even decades after the end of the civil war. Virginia, where Katherine later went to work, was a Confederate state.

Coming from West Virginia, as Katherine did, meant coming from a state where people of different skin colours generally got along together. West Virginia was a mountainous state, with wooded river valleys, rushing rivers and wild, beautiful landscapes. It had broken away from the Confederate state, Virginia, during the American Civil War. Even so, segregation was here, too.

In 1863, the state constitution of West Virginia said there should be a free school system for everyone. Less than ten years later, the law had been changed to say that, "white and coloured persons shall not be taught in the same school." In practice, that meant the best schools, with the best equipment and facilities, were reserved for white children. Black American children got the schools with broken equipment, with holes in the roof and out-of-date textbooks. Moreover, schools in Katherine's birthplace of White Sulphur Springs only provided education for black American students until the eighth grade by this time. It didn't matter how bright a student was or how keen they were to gain qualifications and get a good job: segregation laws meant that if you were black, you stopped getting an education at thirteen. By age ten, Katherine had finished all the work that the school could give her. She was three years ahead of her peers, and hungry to learn more, especially about mathematics.

She recalled:

"YOU'RE EITHER RIGHT OR YOU'RE WRONG. THAT I LIKED ABOUT IT."

A Hundred Miles to School

Katherine's mother and father were not prepared to put up with the limits society tried to impose on them. They believed their children had as much right to learn as anyone. So the Coleman family moved over one hundred miles away, renting a house in another town so that Katherine and her siblings could carry on going to school. It was a big risk, leaving behind everything they had ever known.

The high school Katherine attended was on the campus of West Virginia State University. This college (the equivalent of a British university) had been created to give black students an education, as most colleges refused to allow black students to attend. For Katherine, studying at this school was a great opportunity, because of the link to the college. But moving came with challenges.

Many people in West Virginia were farmers, and although they had owned enslaved people to work the land, there were no big slave owning families. Across the border in Virginia, however, powerful families had enslaved hundreds of people. As a former Confederate state, even decades after slavery had been abolished, Virginia maintained harsh laws to stop black Americans having equal rights with white Americans.

Despite these setbacks, Katherine loved her new school. She developed an interest in space while walking home with the principal one night, who pointed out stars and constellations. Another favourite teacher was Angie Turner King, who had been one of the first black American women to gain a degree in maths and chemistry, at a time when very few women, whatever their colour, had degrees at all. Katherine remembered Mrs King as "bright, caring and very rigorous". That was exactly the kind of teacher that Katherine needed: someone who would mentor her but could also keep up with, and keep challenging, her intelligence.

ANGIE TURNER KING

Angie Turner King was one of Katherine's most influential teachers during high school and at college.

- Born in 1905, in a segregated mining community in West Virginia.
- Her grandparents had been born into slavery.
- Both her parents died when she was young, and she lived with her grandmother who verbally abused her for having dark skin.
- She grew up in great poverty. Her home was so run down that, in the winter, snow would blow in through the broken windows and settle on her bed.
- When she moved to live with her grandfather he made sure that she went to school, where she got good grades and graduated at the age of fourteen from high school.
- By working as a waitress and washing dishes, she paid her way through teacher training school and then college. In 1927, she became one of the first black American women to graduate with a BSc in chemistry and mathematics.

- In 1931 she earned an MSc. from Cornell University
- In 1946 she married. She went on to have five daughters.
- In 1955 she earned a PhD in Mathematics from the University of Pittsburgh.
- Angie Turner King died in 2004 after a long and inspirational career as a scientist and educator. Katherine Johnson called her a "wonderful teacher".

What Does a Research Mathematician Do?

Katherine sped through the work that she was given at high school. She completed all the work they could give her ahead of schedule, once again. In 1936, aged eighteen, she started at West Virginia State University. One of her tutors there was William Waldron Schieffelin Claytor. In 1933 – the same year that Adolf Hitler took power in Germany – Professor Schieffelin Claytor had become the third black American to gain a PhD in mathematics. Katherine enjoyed his classes. His teaching was sometimes difficult for other students to follow, so Katherine often helped them out by asking questions. Professor Schieffelin Claytor told her that he expected her to know the answers. Eventually Katherine confessed that she did know the answers, but that he was losing some of the other students in the room!

Professor Schieffelin Claytor was one of Katherine's most influential teachers. He was determined that she should become a research mathematician. Katherine was fascinated by the idea, but what did a research mathematician do?

"That is for you to find out," the professor replied.

"But where will I find a job?" Katherine asked. She knew that there were only a handful of female mathematicians working in the whole of the country. Moreover, she knew that universities openly discriminated against Irish and Jewish people with a mathematics degree. What hope was there for a black American woman, no matter how smart?

The professor more-or-less shrugged. While she was at college, he persisted in preparing Katherine for a career that seemed as likely to exist, in real life, as a unicorn. Perhaps he simply liked a challenge, or maybe he thought that prejudice against black Americans would have lessened by the time Katherine graduated.

At any rate, if such a job opportunity ever came knocking, he was going to make sure that his star pupil was ready to answer the door. He designed a course on the geometry of space especially for her, and encouraged her to take every mathematics course available. Katherine followed his advice and signed up for heaps of classes, even though it sometimes meant that she was the only student on the course!

WILLIAM WALDRON SCHIEFFELIN CLAYTOR

Professor Schieffelin Claytor was the third black American to earn a PhD in mathematics, and an important person in Katherine Johnson's life.

- Born in 1908. His father was a dentist.
- Went to school in Washington, DC, and later, in Virginia.
- Went to Howard University, a historically black university.
- Awarded a bachelor's degree in maths in 1929.
- Awarded a master's degree in 1930.
- In 1933, achieved his PhD, in topology (the study of the shape of land and surfaces).
- Taught at West Virginia State College (now known as West Virginia State University). One of his students was Katherine Johnson.
- In 1936, did postdoctoral research at the University of Michigan. His colleagues lobbied for him to be offered a permanent job there, but it was refused on the basis of his race.
- In 1947, returned to Howard University to teach. During his career, he gave well-received

presentations at the national meetings of the American Mathematical Society, but he was rejected for opportunities because of his race. He was also not allowed to stay in the hotels where the meetings were being held. Long before the internet, these conferences were how university professors met each other, learned about each other's work and heard about job opportunities. Because he was not allowed to stay in the hotels where the conferences were held, he found himself left out of conversations and opportunities. He eventually stopped attending the conferences altogether.

- Died in 1967.

Advance the Race

Katherine joined the sorority (a society for female students) Alpha Kappa Alpha while at college.

This was the first sorority formed by and for black American women. She remained an active member of the society all her life, supporting young black women in achieving their goals. Many black Americans living under segregation felt a strong sense of responsibility to "advance the race". They felt they had to mentor and support each other because of the many obstacles that society put in their way. Organizations such as the National Association for the Advancement of Colored People (NAACP) fought not just to win single discrimination cases but also to use these cases to change the law for everyone. They wanted equal rights to be upheld in a court of law.

FRATERNITIES AND SORORITIES

At American universities, there are social clubs known as fraternities (for male students) and sororities (for female students). Within these networks, students can make friends and form contacts for life, helping them to secure jobs and opportunities in the future. Because black Americans were banned from joining existing fraternities or sororities they had to start their own. Alpha Kappa Alpha (many fraternities and sororities are referred to by Greek letters) was the first sorority for black American women and was founded in 1908.

If you were forming a fraternity or a sorority, what would its purpose be?

THE NATIONAL ASSOCIATION FOR THE ADVANCEMENT OF COLORED PEOPLE (NAACP)

The NAACP was a group of mostly black lawyers who fought for the legal rights of black Americans. They took unjust cases to court, to force states to comply with the law of the country. Without their actions, equal rights would never have been achieved. Jewish lawyers also fought for civil rights alongside black people.

Katherine graduated from college in 1937, far ahead of her peers, with a bachelor's degree in mathematics and French. Today, someone with her ability would be expected to undertake further studies on postgraduate programmes, but in 1937, West Virginia's postgraduate schools were not open to black students. Katherine left college and began working as a schoolteacher. It was what she had expected all along. "You could be a nurse, or a teacher," she recalled – if you were lucky enough to have had an education, that was.

Having qualifications might get you a better job than working as a servant, but it didn't mean you could get the sort of job that white men got. A black woman just wasn't going to get a job as a research mathematician.

Katherine had never really felt a sense of being discriminated against, until she took on the role as a schoolteacher at a school in Virginia. In Virginia, as in many other states, the buses were segregated. Black people were forced to sit at the back, out of sight of the white people who sat at the front. As soon as Katherine's bus crossed the state line, it came to a stop. The driver told all the black people to move to the back. Katherine was shocked. She refused to move until the driver asked politely. It was important to win the small battles – like turning an order into a request.

WHY WERE BUSES IMPORTANT IN THE CIVIL RIGHTS MOVEMENT?

Because of the size of the USA, many people had to travel long distances for work or to see their families. They travelled on buses, which were like British coaches – they went long distances and stopped in places trains didn't. They were run by private companies who created their own rules about segregation. Bus companies refused to hire black drivers, insisted that black passengers sit at the back of the bus and give up their seat if a white person wanted it. In two separate incidents in 1955, a fifteen year old, Claudette Colvin, and an adult, Rosa Parks, were arrested for refusing to give up their bus seats to a white person. They were not the only two people to resist segregation in this way. After a boycott of the bus company hit them in their pocket, the bus companies were forced to change their prejudiced rules.

Claudette Colvin

Rosa Parks

A Wedding and a War

· ·

1939 was a very important year for the world. Over in Europe, Nazi-led Germany invaded Poland. That was the start of World War II, which would become the biggest and deadliest conflict in human history, and would lead to the murder of six million Jewish people (and other minorities). But in West Virginia, USA, in the beginning, World War II seemed very far away to most Americans. It was a foreign problem.

1939 was also a very important year for Katherine. She had met a chemistry teacher named James "Jimmy" Francis Goble on her first teaching assignment. They married that year. However, she and her husband did not move in together or tell anyone they were married. Partly, this was because Katherine's father had been unenthusiastic about the relationship. He liked Jimmy, but he wanted Katherine to be "something greater" than an elementary school teacher. He wanted her to go to graduate school. He thought that the responsibilities that came with marriage, such as raising children and keeping a home, would stop Katherine from doing that. Another reason for not telling anyone was that Katherine wanted to remain teaching. Wives were not expected to work – their role was supposed to be staying at home and taking care of their husband's needs. If she announced she was married, Katherine's job might have been given to a man. She and Jimmy were determined to do as well as they could as a team – and that meant both of their jobs were important. Katherine prepared for a life as a teacher and a wife. But 1939 proved to be a life-changing year for her in other ways. Completely out of the blue, she was invited to be one of the first three black students to enter West Virginia State University's graduate programme.

All over the USA, schools, colleges and universities were desegregating, admitting black American students for the first time: Black schools also now had to admit white students. This big change had not come about easily: many schools had to be forced to desegregate, often by the NAACP taking them to court. West Virginia State University had faced its own lawsuit.

When a young black man was refused entry into their law school, he promptly took the case to court, with the view to suing the graduate school. The president of the graduate school, worried by the prospect of an expensive lawsuit, bargained. He promised that he would begin to desegregate the graduate school at once, if the young man withdrew his lawsuit. True to his word, the president of West Virginia State University asked the principal of the college to send him "three good students". The principal thought at once of the intelligent young woman who had raced through her work and graduated with the highest honours. He drove to the school where Katherine was working to talk to her about the opportunity. How did she feel about continuing her studies of mathematics at an even higher level?

WORK IS A JOY

Flying High

"I was thrilled!" Katherine said in a later interview, about the offer of a place at graduate school. "It suited me just fine." As much as she enjoyed being a teacher, her real passion was for studying and learning, researching mathematics. Now she was going to get the chance to do what she loved and stretch her mind. Better still, her tuition fees would be paid for her. At a time when it was difficult for most black Americans to get even basic primary schooling, the opportunity to go to graduate school must have seemed like a kind of miracle, albeit one Katherine deserved and had worked hard for.

The opportunity did not come without drawbacks, however. In Katherine's words, "It was not going to be easy!" She would be the only black woman on the campus. Integrating could be dangerous – not everyone was ready for change. Katherine's mother came to stay with her during the summer term to offer moral support.

In 1939, West Virginia State University also became the first historically black college to be allowed to open an aviation programme. World War II had just begun and the USA was under pressure to build up a powerful air force. America was aware that they might need everyone – even black Americans – to serve their country.

Katherine was going to study the science of flight. Aviation was still a very new technology in 1939, and Katherine was excited to be around planes and pilots. She would probably have known about Bessie Coleman, the first black American woman to gain a pilot's licence in 1921.

BESSIE COLEMAN

Bessie Coleman was born in 1892. She was from a very poor family. She managed to save up enough money from working to pay for a term at university and later heard about flying from some men who had been pilots in World War I. She managed to get funding from a black-owned newspaper to travel to Paris to learn to fly an aeroplane, as nowhere in the USA would train a black woman to fly. Because of her race she could not find work as a commercial pilot, so she had to become a stunt flyer, who performed aerial tricks – figure of 8s, and loop-the-loops – for audiences in a small biplane, called a Curtis JN-1. She wanted to set up a school for black aviators, but never had the chance. In 1926, at the age of 34, she died in a crash caused by a mechanic who had left his wrench in the plane's engine. Her incredible achievements inspired many black men and women to take up flying.

Katherine's time at graduate school was made as easy as possible by supportive tutors. Most of the staff members and students were friendly. The one student who objected to sharing the course with a black woman simply ignored her, rather than directly abusing her. The work was fascinating. However, by the end of the summer term, Katherine found out that she was pregnant. That meant that she and Jimmy could no longer hide their marriage. It also meant – because of the expectations placed on mothers at that time – that she had to leave the graduate programme. A single woman might go to graduate school, but a mother was expected to make looking after her children and husband her full-time job.

News from Newport News

Having to leave graduate school almost as soon as she had started was a disappointment, but Katherine loved family life, so it did not feel like such a big sacrifice. She would go on to have three children with Jimmy: Joylette, Katherine and

Constance. When the children were old enough, she returned to teaching maths, French and music in schools in Virginia and West Virginia. Perhaps it wasn't exactly the work she had wanted, but Katherine had always believed it was important to:

"DO YOUR BEST, AT ALL TIMES."

It was a motto she now applied to her domestic life and to teaching, just as she had applied it to her studies.

Teaching did not pay much money. Black American teachers were paid less than white teachers, and even the white teachers in Virginia were paid some of the lowest salaries in the USA. Teachers were expected to do a lot, from cleaning out their classrooms to making lunch for their pupils. Schools for black American children were poorly funded, and some rural schools had simply closed during the Great Depression, leaving a generation of black Americans without education. Katherine made her salary stretch by saving wherever she could. She sewed clothes for her family rather than buying them. During the summer, she and her husband worked as "help" (live-in housekeepers) for a rich family who spent the holidays in the mountains nearby. Working two jobs and keeping a household going was not easy, but there were few other options.

It was not until several years later, when perhaps it seemed to Katherine that she would be a teacher for as long as she lived, that a family wedding changed everything.

In August 1952, Katherine and Jimmy travelled to Virginia to attend the wedding of Jimmy's younger sister. Also at the wedding were Jimmy's other sister, Margaret Epps, and her husband Eric. Eric, it turned out, had some very interesting news for them.

Today, with access to the internet and mobile phones always at our fingertips, it is easy to forget what life must have been like in the days when telephones were still a luxury. Sometimes people would go months without speaking to their relatives, only reuniting at special occasions like weddings or funerals. As a result, Eric's news came as a total surprise. He told Katherine and Jimmy that there was work going where he lived. Work that sounded a lot more interesting than teaching. Work that sounded exactly right for Katherine.

"Why don't you come home with us? I can get you both jobs," Eric said to Katherine and Jimmy.

The National Advisory Committee for Aeronautics (NACA)

Eric and Margaret lived in Newport News, Virginia. The jobs Eric was thinking of for Katherine was at the National Advisory Committee for Aeronautics (NACA). NACA's purpose was to research and develop aviation. They had a laboratory in nearby Langley, Virginia. There, scientists, mathematicians and engineers worked on making planes better, stronger, faster and more powerful. The NACA employees made the planes safer for those who flew them – people like the young airmen who had studied on the same campus as Katherine at graduate school – and more dangerous for the USA's enemies. At Langley, researchers developed new wing shapes that reduced drag, discovered mathematical rules that made flying more efficient and created a super-compressor that enabled planes to fly at supersonic speeds. The particular job that Eric had in mind for Katherine was not exactly the academic career that Professor Schieffelin Claytor had dreamed of, but it was close. It was maths work. If she was hired, Katherine's job title would be "computer". Computers worked out complex mathematical problems. Mostly they did this in their heads, although there were mechanical desk calculators to help them and NACA bought its first electronic calculator in 1947. Langley was a busy, noisy place with its own airfield and wind tunnel, where a mathematician would be able to see the practical results of their calculations every day. To Katherine, it sounded not only interesting, but exciting, too!

WIND TUNNELS

How do you test out a new aeroplane wing, without risking anyone's life? Test pilots can take fully built planes up in the sky, but an aeroplane is made up of many complicated bits which all have to be designed, built and tested before they can be assembled. A wind tunnel is like an enormous fan, big enough for an aeroplane to be put into. Safely on the ground, engineers can see how wings, fuselage and engines perform, and perfect them before building them into a test plane.

NACA had actually been hiring female mathematicians since 1935. At first, people had been doubtful, but they soon got used to the women's presence, accepting that they were good at their jobs. Besides, it made financial sense. Women were classified as sub-professional workers and could be paid less than men. Then, during World War II, there was a shortage of workers.

The war created a lot of well-paid work, in industry as well as the armed forces. At first, however, these well-paid jobs were reserved for white people.

Asa Philip Randolph, a civil rights leader, threatened to lead a protest march if war jobs were not opened to black people. The President, Franklin D. Roosevelt, gave in. He signed executive orders, opening war jobs to black Americans. In 1943, NACA began to hire black women to do maths. They were placed in a separate, segregated department for black American female computers, called the West Area Computing Unit.

In 1952, the department was still going strong, and Eric thought that Katherine was a perfect candidate. Eric was sure he could find Jimmy work too, on the docks at Newport News. It was better paid than working as a teacher had been – and it meant Katherine could take up this exciting chance to do a professional job that very few black women ever got to do at this time in the USA.

Years earlier, Katherine's family had made a big move for the sake of education. Now, Katherine and Jimmy had to decide whether they should quit their jobs and uproot their young children for the chance to work at NACA. Moving to an unknown area could be dangerous. Housing was segregated, and neighbours would be sure to make their feelings known if Katherine and Jimmy wound up in the wrong area. It was a risk – but a risk that they decided to take. They moved to the coastal city of Newport News, one of the oldest European settlements in the USA and a famous ship-building town.

Katherine and Dorothy

Eric introduced Katherine to one of the supervisors of the West Area Computing Unit – another black woman, a few years older than Katherine, named Dorothy Vaughan. It turned out that the two women had already met. In 1942, Dorothy had accompanied her husband to White Sulphur Springs. He had worked at the Greenbrier Hotel, which was then being used as an internment camp for German, Italian and some Japanese officials. In White Sulphur Springs, the Vaughans had met Joshua and Joylette Coleman, Katherine's parents. They had got on well, and Dorothy's children had come to see Mr and Mrs Coleman as a kind of extra set of grandparents. Katherine and Dorothy had met briefly when Katherine came home from teaching school, but after that their ways had parted. In 1943, while Katherine had been raising a young family, Dorothy had got a job in the West Area Computing Unit. Now, ten years later, Dorothy was the first black person to be head of that department – indeed, the first black head of any NACA department.

DOROTHY VAUGHAN

- Born in 1910.
- Awarded a degree in mathematics from Wilberforce University in 1929.
- Married Howard Vaughan in 1932 and went on to have six children.
- Offered the opportunity to study at Howard University, but decided to work as a teacher instead as she needed a steady income. She knew that if she took a further degree, racism would prevent her from finding a job.
- Began working as a mathematician and programmer at NACA in 1943.
- Became acting head of the segregated West Area Computing Unit in 1949, making her the first black head of a division. She calculated flight paths, including for rockets, and taught herself how to program using Fortran language, knowing that this would be essential to keep her job.

- Lost her position as a head of department when the West Area Computing Unit was dissolved in 1958. Despite her many skills, there was nowhere else she could be promoted to, because white men and women would not accept a superior who was black.
- Died in 2008.

"I CHANGED WHAT I COULD, AND WHAT I COULDN'T, I ENDURED."

Dorothy and Katherine had lots in common. They were both mothers, teachers, members of Alpha Kappa Alpha and their maths abilities had let them skip ahead several grades at school. Dorothy told Katherine, "They're not hiring right now, but I will get you an application and put your name forward."

In 1952, Katherine sent in an application to join the West Area Computing Unit – and hoped. In the meantime, she worked as a substitute teacher. In June of 1952, NACA contacted her with a job offer. At the same time, she was offered a permanent teaching job. Once again Katherine had to choose between something familiar and reliable – teaching – and something new and risky. And yet to Katherine there was no real competition – not even when the school offered to match the much higher salary that the government would pay her at NACA.

"Well," Katherine said. "I came here [to Newport News] to be a research mathematician. I think I'll try that one first!"

Two workplaces wanted her, and one was even willing to raise her salary to keep her – this was something for Katherine to be quietly, solidly proud of. Having choice meant having power, and having power meant she might – despite oppression and prejudice – be able to improve her life and her children's futures. Not just that, but by showing people what she was capable of, she could change what people believed black women in general were capable of. She could change the future for everyone, for the better.

Starting Work

Katherine began to work at Langley in 1953. In her previous workplace, a school for black children staffed by black teachers, she had been able to ignore segregation to an extent. Now that she was employed in a mixed workplace, there was no escaping the signs directing her to the "Colored Girls" bathroom, or to the segregated table where the West Area Computing Unit had to sit to eat. In an unfair world, it was important to pick your battles. To Katherine, workplace segregation was not something she was going to waste energy worrying about. Instead, she focused on her work. As she said, "I was finally going to find out what a research mathematician did!"

*

So, what did a mathematician do in the West Area Computing Unit in 1953? The department was made up of a "pool" of thirteen women, and if an engineer needed a mathematician, they simply requested one to work on their project.

"They [the engineers] just wanted someone to do the little stuff," Katherine recalled, with a grin. "While they did the thinking!"

The women were assigned to do jobs that electronic computers do today. They ran through seemingly endless data lists on huge piles of paper, following narrow rows of figures and doing the calculations that the engineers needed done. "It was fascinating to me," Katherine recalled. And she was already one step ahead: her principal at school had a mechanical desk calculator, so she had used one before. These machines were the size of desktop computers today.

There were no men in the computing pool.

Engineering – rough, tough and more physical – was seen as a man's job. In 1953, when Katherine first started working at NACA, there were no black engineers being hired.

When the first black engineers were finally taken on in 1964, Katherine recalled that they had "a hard time" conquering their colleagues' prejudices. By comparison, the black, female mathematicians were popular. They were often more capable than the white female mathematicians. While a white woman might get a job in the computing pool just by knowing an influential person within NACA, the black computers had to prove their worth with college degrees and hard work. Despite the pressure, Katherine thrived in a workplace where it really mattered whether the sums were right – because her sums were always right.

IT TAKES A WAR TO CHANGE THE WORLD

In Britain, during World War I, thousands of men were conscripted into the army and sent overseas to fight, leaving few men at home to do essential jobs like working in weapons factories or farming. Women began doing these jobs and proved they could do them well. They gained new skills and financial independence. After World War I, the government tried to take these roles away from women and give them back to men. But women fought to keep their jobs – and employers now knew that a woman could do them just as well as a man. Similarly, World War II led to black Americans taking on jobs they had never been allowed to do before. Again, once the war was over, the government tried give these jobs back to white people. Black people fought to keep their careers, money and independence, and white employers were now more likely to think that the colour bar made no sense. After all, black Americans were good at their jobs, so why shouldn't they be employed? The world wars, destructive as they were, led to steps forward in equality for women and people of colour.

MASSIVE RESISTANCE

Crash

••

Katherine didn't stay in the computing pool for long. Just two weeks into her new job, an engineer asked for two computers to work in the Flight Research Division. Dorothy Vaughan sent Katherine. Katherine was good at her work – so good that the engineers never returned her to the computing pool. She remained attached to the Flight Research Division. For Katherine, that meant an opportunity to be around the "thinking". Working alongside white, male engineers, she was able to develop a specialism, and that made her a very valuable colleague. The engineers were not about to reject someone for being a different colour, or a woman, if they could do the mathematics. And Katherine could clearly do the mathematics.

Katherine's curiosity and intelligence made

her a great fit for the Flight Research Division at NACA. One of her jobs was to read the contents of "black boxes", the data-recording equipment inside aeroplanes, used to determine the cause of a crash. In one case, a small propeller plane had crashed for no apparent reason – it had simply fallen out of the sky. Katherine was fascinated. What had happened? There was always a cause. She discovered that a jet plane had passed in the air above the small plane some time before. This meant the air remained disturbed from the jet's movement – just as a boat leaves the water choppy long after it has disappeared over the horizon. The research she was involved in led to changes in aviation rules that would stop an accident like that happening ever again.

But just as Katherine's career was going better than she could ever have hoped for, a crash came out of the blue sky in her personal life. Her husband, Jimmy, had not been well for a long time. He was eventually diagnosed with a brain tumour. Tragically, the tumour could not be operated on. In 1956, at the age of just forty-three, Katherine's husband died.

NACA'S GREATEST ACHIEVEMENTS

1920s: invented the NACA cowling, a cover for aircraft engines that made them more efficient and safer.

1930s: developed a new way to design aerofoils (the cross-section of aircraft wings) that became used all over the world.

1930s: discovered – and photographed – the shockwave (an event that stops aircraft crossing the sound barrier easily).

1940s: created the Bell X-1, the first plane to break the sound barrier.

Jimmy's death must have been devastating for Katherine, who had not only lost the person she loved, but now had to raise their three children alone. The area they lived in, Newsome Park – known as "the projects" – had been built as segregated housing for black people. It was constantly under threat of demolition by the state of Virginia. Jimmy and Katherine had always planned to move out so that their daughters had better opportunities – somewhere they wouldn't have to worry that their home could be knocked down at any moment. But without Jimmy, the dream of moving to a better area was suddenly out of reach.

Pushing the Limits

However, it just wasn't in Katherine's nature to give up. She made sure that the principal at her daughters' school did not lower his expectations of them out of sympathy. "They are going to college, and they need to be prepared," Katherine told him. She instructed her daughters to take care of the house and to have the evening meal ready for when she got home. They were relying on one income now. She was like a mountaineer who had lost her climbing partner. She was still climbing – she had her eyes on the summit – but she knew that a single wrong step could send her tumbling down. There was no safety net and no one to rescue her. Everything depended on her keeping her job. Luckily, she loved her work, and she was brilliant at it. As she would say later in life:

"I LIKED WHAT I WAS DOING... I LIKED WORK... IT WAS A JOY..."

NACA was a busy, noisy and exciting place to be. Katherine was working with engineers who were pushing the boundaries of aviation, making aeroplanes fly faster than ever before. The onsite airfield reminded Katherine of the real impact her work had on the test pilots who flew the planes. She was surrounded by intelligent people who liked the fact that she asked questions. She felt comfortable in the Flight Research Department.

AERODYNAMICS: THE SCIENCE OF FLIGHT

Aerodynamics is the science of how air behaves around solid objects. Scientists apply the principles of aerodynamics when they are working out how to make aeroplanes fly further, faster and more efficiently.

THE FOUR FORCES OF FLIGHT:

Lift describes the force that pushes the object upwards. Aeroplane wings are designed to get a lot of lift.

Drag is the force of air that acts against the object, stopping it from moving forwards.

Thrust is the force that pushes the object forwards. Thrust is produced by the engines of an aeroplane.

Weight is the force that pushes the object down towards Earth. Thrust and lift have to overcome drag and weight to get an aeroplane off the runway and flying through the air.

Katherine kept herself busy outside of work, too. She attended church and remained involved in Alpha Kappa Alpha. Langley was buzzing with social activities, free lectures and night-school courses. Most of these were open to black employees as well as white. Despite the troubles of the 1940s and 1950s, everyone in the department generally got on well with each other, whatever their skin colour. They all shared a passion for research and pushing flight to its limits. What would be next? What barriers would be broken, what things that had seemed impossible would turn out to be possible? That was the excitement of working somewhere like Langley: you saw things getting better and problems being slowly but surely solved. Progress was visible, every single day.

GLAMOROUS GLENNIS

Chuck Yeagar

SUBSONIC, TRANSONIC, SUPERSONIC AND HYPERSONIC... WHAT DOES IT ALL MEAN?

Sound travels in waves. These waves travel at different speeds depending on certain conditions:

how wet or dry it is, what temperature it is and what material the sound is travelling through. The way sound waves behave is complicated, but not random. Their behaviour can be explained and predicted by mathematics.

The speed of sound in air is generally taken to be 343 metres (1,125 ft) per second (but this can be affected by several different variables including temperature). When an object passes the speed of sound, there is a loud noise. You don't need an aircraft to experience this sound. Just watch an old cowboy film. The crack of the whip is the sound the tip makes as it passes, or "breaks", the sound barrier.

Subsonic = below the speed of sound.

Transonic = speeds around – just before and just after – the speed of sound.

Supersonic = speeds that are faster than sound.

Hypersonic = speeds that are even faster than that!

For a long time, people thought that it was impossible to travel faster than the speed of sound. Then Chuck Yeager, flying an X-1 experimental aeroplane developed at NACA, proved them wrong by breaking the sound barrier. It turned out that when an aircraft went at the speed of sound, there was an explosion of sound waves – a "sonic boom". Just before you got to this speed, and just after you passed it, is known as the transonic speed. At these speeds, sound waves behave in very complicated ways. The equations to explain and predict how they behave are equally complicated. That was why NACA bought its electronic calculator in 1947.

The Forces of Resistance

But even with these advances in technology, times were troubled. The civil rights movement was gathering power and pace, but those opposing it were pushing back relentlessly. Some states simply refused to comply with laws enforcing equality. These states wanted to maintain white supremacy and force separation between black and white people. Children were often on the frontline of the battle. In 1951, students at Robert Russa Moton High School, where Dorothy Vaughan had taught, walked out in protest at the terrible conditions at their school.

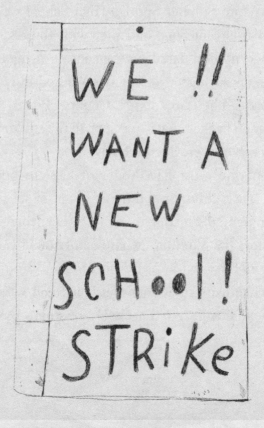

The NAACP took the case to the Supreme Court. In 1954, the Supreme Court ruled that there should be an end to segregation in schools. But just because the law had changed, it didn't mean that powerful politicians across the USA would obey it.

In West Virginia most schools desegregated quietly. But in Greenbrier County, where Katherine had gone to elementary school, there were ugly protests. Black children who tried to go to White Sulphur Springs High School were barred from entering, and met with threats of violence if they dared set foot inside it, along with signs saying, "No Negroes Wanted in Our Schools". The Greenbrier County Board of Education backed down and sent all the students back to their segregated schools.

Katherine must have found it hard to hear about black children being forced out of school in her hometown, but there were even bigger problems in Virginia, where she now lived. Senator Harry Byrd was the governor of Virginia and he refused to accept that black and white children should go to school together. Byrd wanted Virginia to stay segregated. He called his strategy "massive resistance". Byrd closed the schools in Virginia altogether rather than let black children enter them. Racism kept both white and black children at home. One white parent said that he would rather his children lived in ignorance than go to school with black children.

MASSIVE RESISTANCE

"If we can organize the Southern States for massive resistance to this order I think that in time the rest of the country will realize that racial integration is not going to be accepted in the South." – Senator Harry F. Byrd.

In 1954, Byrd and 100 other politicians from southern states (those which had fought to keep slaves during the American Civil War) signed a document saying that they refused to stop segregating their schools. They passed laws designed to stop schools integrating (teaching black and white children together) and to destroy those schools that did integrate. First, lawmakers prevented integrated schools from having funding, and gave the state the power to close schools that dared to integrate. A second law said that a group of officials should decide where children should go to school – and these officials made sure to separate them by race.

A third law took the money that would have gone to closed, integrated schools, and used it to pay people to send their children to segregated private schools.

Some black teachers were nervous about integration, too. They knew that many white parents would refuse to let their children be taught by black teachers, and feared that they would lose their jobs as a result.

> Massive Resistance eventually failed, but hundreds of children, both black and white, had had their education disrupted and stolen from them in the process.

Elsewhere in the USA, efforts to desegregate schools were being met with furious, racist resistance. In Little Rock, Arkansas, in 1957, a group of nine black teenagers tried to attend a white school in accordance with the new laws. In response, the state called out the National Guard – a kind of police force – to stop them. The teenagers found their entry to school blocked by armed men, as if they were dangerous criminals. The federal government had to bring in the army to escort them into school.

In 1960, in New Orleans, Ruby Bridges, a six-year-old girl, walked to school under armed guard. A crowd had gathered outside the school, waiting for her. They threw things and shouted threats. When she entered the school, white parents took their children home, refusing to

let them be taught with her. All but one of the teachers refused to have her in their class. For a year, Ruby was taught alone, as if she had a contagious disease. Her family were bullied and threatened for daring to send her to school.

Katherine had been forced to move for her education. Her own three children went to a segregated school in Virginia. Katherine must have wondered if her grandchildren, too, would go to a segregated school. How could it be easier to break the sound barrier than to break the barrier of segregation?

A Cold War

Internationally, too, things had never looked so frightening for ordinary American people. World War II had ended in 1945 with a terrible new weapon, capable of flattening cities and killing hundreds of thousands of people in one blow, called the atomic bomb. America had dropped two of these bombs on the Japanese cities of Hiroshima and Nagasaki. Around 146,000 people died in Hiroshima and 80,000 in Nagasaki.

During World War II, the USA was the only country in the world that had atomic bombs, with enough materials to make nine of these weapons. But by the late 1950s, both the Soviet Union – a group of countries, including Russia, under a Communist rule – and the USA had hundreds of nuclear weapons, some of which were much more powerful than those dropped on Hiroshima and Nagasaki. The Soviet Union detonated its first nuclear bomb in 1949. A deadly race began between the Soviet Union and the USA, each striving to become the country with the greatest number of powerful nuclear weapons. At the same time, politicians were desperate not to turn the rivalry, known as the Cold War, hot. If the USA dropped a bomb on a Soviet city, or vice versa, the other country could send a bomb back to them in seconds. It was one thing to own these weapons, but actually using them would lead to World War III. Such a war would cause so much death and destruction that it would probably be the last war the world ever had. There was a serious chance that humans would be wiped out. The Cold War was a standoff, where neither country could afford to use their weapons, but neither could afford to lose power, either.

THE COLD WAR

The Cold War was known by this name because the two powers involved, the Soviet Union and the USA, never fought each other directly. After the end of World War II, the USA and the Soviet Union were the two most powerful nations in the world were. Their governments had very different ideas about how the world should be run. They did not like each other's ideas. They became rivals, competing for power and influence. Although the two nations never went to war with each other directly, they built and hoarded nuclear weapons and got involved in other wars around the world to try to gain power. To many people, the Cold War meant the constant threat of a nuclear bomb dropping out of the sky on to their heads. As much as the Soviet Union and the USA were rivals, politicians on both sides realized that if a nuclear war started, no one would win. They spent a lot of time trying to make sure that they did not push each other into sending the first nuclear missile. Eventually, the Soviet Union dissolved into separate countries.

Small Victories

The rivalry with Communist Russia led to a fear of anything that upset the way of life most Americans were used to. That included women's rights, equality for black people and desegregation. This fear affected NACA, too. In 1951, Matilda West, a relative of Dorothy Vaughan's and an active campaigner for equal rights, was fired from her job as a computer. NACA's message was clear – if you didn't keep your head down, if you were a little bit too loud about wanting equal rights, you might lose your job. If you had a family to feed, as Katherine did, it was not a risk you wanted to take.

However, Katherine found her own ways to deal with prejudice. For example, there were no "Colored Girls" bathroom signs in the Flight Research Division because no black Americans were expected to be there. Katherine simply used whichever bathroom she wanted to, and no one objected. She ate lunch at her desk to avoid the segregation in the cafeteria. Just as she had always done, Katherine picked her battles. She was breaking barriers every day, just by being who she was and working where she did.

The most important work that the division did was to create research reports – written documents with information about new discoveries. The engineers discussed these reports at regular meetings – but women did not go to the meetings. The more time Katherine spent in the department, the less sense this seemed to make. She needed to know what was going on and she could do a better job if she understood what was happening in the meetings.

"Why can't I go to the meetings?" she asked.

"Girls don't go to the meetings," was the reply.

"Is there a law against it?" she asked.

There was not. So Katherine kept on asking and asking and asking until, finally, the engineers gave in.

Katherine took her place in the meeting, and she was never asked to leave. It was reminiscent of the barriers that her mentor, Professor Schiefflin Claytor, had faced when he was refused entry to hotels where conferences were being held. At least Katherine had been able to break this barrier. From now on, women did go to the meetings – she had set a precedent.

GETTING INTO SPACE

Sputnik

∙∙

NACA's experimental aeroplanes were getting closer and closer to space, nudging the edge of Earth's atmosphere, like baby birds nudging against their egg-shells, desperate to spread their wings. But the government told NACA not to waste money on space flight. It wasn't what the country needed, it was expensive and it was hard to achieve. NACA continued to focus their research on developing commercial aircraft to meet the increased desire for transport across the USA and beyond. Safer, bigger and better aeroplanes meant more people could travel and be more connected. In a huge country like the USA, that really mattered. Even people of colour flew, although they were discriminated against throughout the process, often bumped from flights to make space for white passengers, and subjected to segregation at airports. Ironically, Katherine would have been barred from working as a pilot or member of the cabin crew on the same aeroplanes that she was making safer and more efficient through her work at Langley.

Still, space flight was important because of what was happening on Earth. Getting a satellite into orbit was an important step towards having missiles that could fly from continent to continent, from the Soviet Union to America. In 1955, President Eisenhower announced that the USA would launch an artificial satellite in 1958.

Then, Sputnik changed the game.

While the USA had been working to connect the people of the world with aeroplanes, the Soviet Union had been racing to get a satellite into space first. They kept their work secret, so that when they announced they had launched their satellite into orbit, on 4 October 1957, it was a shock for the rest of the world.

The Soviet Union's satellite was called Sputnik 1: a small, polished metal ball, with four long, whisker-like radio antennae. It looked like a seed from some giant alien plant, or a floating sea mine. Animations on American newsreels showed it beeping menacingly. You could see it for yourself if you went outside and looked up at the right time during the night, as the Soviets published a list of the places the satellite would be passing over. Katherine went outside with everyone else and stared up at the flashing pinprick of light from its rocket boosters. While many others saw it as a frightening intrusion by the enemy, Katherine's curious, scientific mind was fascinated. She knew that the USA had been challenged. Sure enough, the next day at work, everyone was talking about it. How could the Soviets have been allowed to vault so far ahead? The NACA scientists were frustrated, certain they could have got a satellite into orbit first if only they had been allowed to try. They discussed ideas and began to make plans. Katherine, in the Flight Research Division, was at the heart of these exciting conversations.

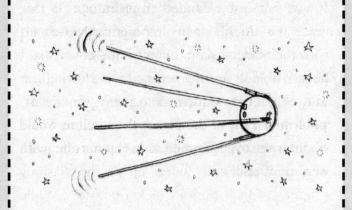

SPUTNIK 1: FACTS AND FIGURES

- Appearance: a shiny silver ball with four long antennae sticking out of it.
- Size: 58 centimetres (23 in.) in diameter.
- Weight: 83.6 kilograms (183.9 lbs).
- Length of time to orbit Earth: ninety-six minutes.
- Time in orbit: three months. After that time, Sputnik 1 burned up falling through the atmosphere.
- Meaning of name: fellow traveller.

It was not just wounded American pride that made it suddenly seem important to catch up with the Soviet Union. Fears of Soviet spies had been whipped up to a fever pitch following the war. Now here, it seemed to many Americans, was a Soviet spy in the sky, watching them. What would it see? What would it do? How vulnerable were they, really?

The Race to Space

Only the USA and the Soviet Union had the technology and resources to develop space travel at this time. Many European powers had been devastated by World War II, along with Japan. The rest of the world was watching to see what the USA's response would be. In the meantime, the Soviet Union pressed on. They sent a dog, Laika, into orbit in 1957 on Sputnik 2. The unfortunate dog only lived a few hours in space, but the message was clear. If you could send a dog into space, you could send a man.

Laika the dog.

ANIMALS IN SPACE

The first living beings humans launched into space were fruit flies! Long before the Soviet Union and USA developed the technology to put satellites in orbit, they sent up rockets containing animals to test the effects of space travel on living things. A group of fruit flies were launched into space in 1947, to study the effects of radiation. The fruit flies

103

were fine, and made it back to Earth alive. Other animals were not so lucky. Mice, dogs, tortoises, monkeys and apes were all sent into space before humans. Most of them did not survive the journey.

The Americans, meanwhile, were struggling to get anything into space at all. A month after the launch of Sputnik 2, they launched their own satellite, Vanguard, on 6 December 1957. It was a spectacular failure. The Vanguard rocket did not get close to orbit before it fell back to Earth, exploding the fuel tanks and destroying the launch pad. The American press had a great time, nicknaming the failed satellite "Flopnik", "Oopsnik" and "Stayputnik". The Soviets had an even better time. Would the USA like to benefit from their aid fund for underdeveloped nations?

Suddenly, space was all anyone was interested in. Nothing else mattered. Questions were being asked in the newspapers and around dinner tables: why was the USA so far behind the Soviet Union in science and technology? More and more people pointed out that the Soviet Union was employing women across its space programme. Was it possible that women were not being used to their full potential in America? And what about black Americans – was it possible that they were being held back by the inefficient segregated education system, and their intelligence wasted? Was it segregation that was making the USA fall behind its rival, the Soviet Union? Black Americans thought that was pretty clear, but now white people were thinking about it too, forced to accept the obvious by the threat of the atomic missiles pointing at them.

America eventually managed to get two satellites, Explorer 1 and Vanguard 1, into orbit in 1958. Still, eight out of the eleven Vanguard launches failed. The USA was in second place, and the heavens belonged to the Soviet Union. But out of that humiliating realization came a new organization – NASA – and the work Katherine Johnson was most proud of: lunar orbit rendezvous.

NASA

The National Aeronautics and Space Act was signed by President Eisenhower in 1958. Like a wave of a magic wand, it turned the agency formerly known as NACA into NASA: the National Aeronautics and Space Administration. Katherine's place of work transformed from the Flight Research Division into the Aerospace Mechanics Division. Now her job was no longer to improve flight, but to make flight beyond the limits of Earth, into space, possible.

President Eisenhower

NASA had plenty of new objectives which boiled down to: get us flying faster, further, better, more safely, and get us into space. One of the objectives underlined the political importance of the work:

"THE PRESERVATION OF THE ROLE OF THE UNITED STATES AS A LEADER IN AERONAUTICAL AND SPACE SCIENCE AND TECHNOLOGY..."

This wasn't just about being the best, this was about being seen to be the best, in the USA and internationally. Television was to play a big part in that. Television, like flight, was not exactly a new invention, but was becoming better, cheaper and available to more and more people. In 1950, only nine per cent of American families had a television but by 1960, it was ninety per cent. Hardly anyone could go down to Cape Canaveral, Florida to see the launch of a rocket, but almost everyone could watch it on television without leaving their house.

DEVELOPMENT OF TELEVISION

The Space Race was never just about space. It was also about Earth. The USA wanted to show the world what it was achieving. Television had developed fast at the start of the twentieth century, transforming from fuzzy, silent movies, to clearer films with sound. Cinemas had grown and multiplied. Television sets small enough to fit into a living room had been invented. Right from the start, American space missions were planned with television in mind. Because if the world didn't see it happen, how would they know it really occurred? You couldn't argue with the camera.

Preparations began for sending an astronaut into space – the first American in space. The project was called Project Mercury, and the first seven men chosen to be astronauts were known as the Mercury Seven. NASA would use a rocket called Atlas to get the capsule up into space.

Around the same time, Katherine met James A Johnson, who had been a second lieutenant in the army and served in the Korean War. They soon began dating and fell in love. Like Jimmy, he was supportive of her work. Unlike the head of her department, Henry Pearson, who was not keen on women in the workplace, James respected and admired Katherine's dedication to her job. And the job was getting even more interesting. Katherine had been given the task of calculating the trajectory that a spacecraft would take as it carried an astronaut into orbit, and then – the tricky bit – down to Earth again.

Getting things into space wasn't so hard. Another department at NACA, the Pilotless Aircraft Research Division, had sent rockets into the air at incredible speeds from their island launch pad off the Virginian coast. They were sure they could send a capsule, and a man, up into orbit with one of their rockets. But what about coming down again?

The Big Challenge

A Space Task Group was set up to work through all the challenges of getting a man into space, and safely back down again. One of the first questions to tackle was: what shape should the craft be? Pointed, aerodynamic objects, like rockets, were good for going up into space quickly. But coming back, when they hit Earth's atmosphere, the forces they passed through were intense. The friction from these forces could cause the spacecraft to burn up like a meteor.

If you were sending an unmanned satellite

into orbit, you didn't need to worry about getting it back down – it would burn up in Earth's atmosphere on re-entry, so nothing large enough to cause a problem would hit the ground. But if you were sending a person up there, you had to find a way of returning them safely to earth. After all, everything would be televised.

The engineers at NASA got busy working out how to create a spacecraft that could return an astronaut safely to Earth. They needed to design something that was somehow pointed going up, but rounded coming down, to reduce the pressures on the object.

Some engineers at NASA had the idea of sending up a kind of aeroplane. It would launch like a rocket and then glide back down again. But that was a whole new kind of space shuttle, and it would take too long to develop. The USA was so far behind already that the government wanted a fast solution.

NASA decided that the best way forward was to have two objects: a fast, pointed, powerful rocket to pierce the atmosphere like an arrow, and a rounded capsule which would be attached to it. The astronaut would be inside the capsule.

The rocket would fall away as soon as it had done its job of lifting the capsule into orbit. The capsule would continue floating in orbit until the astronaut pressed a switch to fire up engines to re-enter the atmosphere gently and come back down to Earth again.

So the engineers had come up with a solution to one problem – but there was another mathematical problem that still needed to be solved. How and when should they launch the spacecraft, and how could they know where and when it would land? Someone had to calculate the trajectory that the spacecraft would follow, taking into account all the different forces that would act on it. It was work that required focus, attention to detail, a strong nerve and a very fast, capable brain for mathematical calculations. Katherine had all these qualities.

To Space – and Back Again!

Putting things into space is one thing. Getting them back again safely is another. When a spacecraft is launched from Earth, it doesn't go up in a straight line. Because of the gravity of the Earth it travels in a curved line. NASA knew that the Project Mercury spacecraft would fly into orbit in a large arc, as if it were hit by a giant tennis racket. Whoever was in the capsule would need to re-enter the atmosphere at exactly the right speed and angle. They would also need to land in exactly the right place. Landing on the ground meant a hard landing; landing in the sea was better, but the capsule could sink. NASA needed to be sure that the capsule would land in an exact location, so that a ship could be there waiting to rescue the astronauts. What made this so difficult was the fact that Earth itself is constantly moving – rotating on its axis and orbiting around the Sun. Also adding to the problem was the fact that Earth is not completely spherical, but squashed (oblate). Putting all the known and unknown factors together into a series of equations, and working out from that when to launch the rocket that would carry the capsule for the first manned Mercury mission, was a highly complex piece of mathematics.

Depending on those equations were billions of dollars of investment, hundreds of jobs and at least one man's life. You would have to be very sure that you were a good mathematician to volunteer for such a job.

"Let me do it," Katherine said to Ted Skopinski, her engineering colleague. Confident and keen, she worked through equation after equation, spending long days and late nights getting it right. Together, she and Ted prepared a research report that would end up with the tongue-tangling title: "Determination of Azimuth Angle at Burnout for Placing a Satellite Over a Selected Earth Position." It was a mathematical description of the method to put a man into space. The report explained how to bring a spacecraft back down to an exact landing place on Earth. It was a mathematical answer to the question: how do we bring our astronauts safely home again?

TRIGONOMETRY: THE SCIENCE OF TRIANGLES

One of the branches of mathematics that Katherine Johnson used a lot is called trigonometry. This is the mathematics of triangles. It is possible to calculate the position and distance of stars, planets and other objects in space using trigonometry.

Trigonometry was developed as early as 300 BC by Greek mathematicians who realized that, if you knew the length of one side of a triangle and the angle of one of its corners, it was possible to work out the other sides and angles mathematically. They used this technique to measure the height of very tall objects like towers or mountains and even to calculate the distance from Earth to the Moon.

As Ted Skopinski took on other projects within the Space Task Group, Katherine found herself in charge of their joint report. Reports were important, because having your name on them meant that you became known for doing your own research and thinking independently. No woman had ever authored a research report from the Aerospace Mechanics Division, or from the Flight Research Division, before. The head of the division, Henry Pearson, did not like working with women. He wanted the reports to come from the male engineers. But the engineers were overwhelmed with the amount of work needed for the Mercury missions. In the end, Ted Skopinski told Henry Pearson that Katherine should finish writing it. "She's done most of the work anyway," he said. Pearson had to agree.

After months of being checked and double-checked, reviewed and critiqued, Ted and Katherine's report was finally published in 1960. Katherine had gone from not being allowed into the meetings, to having her name on an important research paper. "Determination of Azimuth Angle at Burnout for Placing a Satellite over a Selected Earth Position" was many things. It was the first research report with a female author to come out of that department at NASA. It was a mathematical description of how to get a man back safely from space. It was a record of her new name, as in 1959 while writing the report, Katherine had married James A. Johnson. And it was an undeniable record that she, Katherine Johnson, a black American woman, was a crucial part of America's biggest and most exciting national project ever. Whether it liked it or not, America could not do without women like her.

SEEING THE FUTURE

In the 1960s, science fiction stories about threatening aliens were popular. But so was science fiction about humans exploring space and living in peace with people from other planets. *Star Trek* broke barriers, linking space travel to progressive ideas. The character of Lieutenant Uhura, played by

Nichelle Nichols, meant there was a competent, intelligent black woman aboard the *Enterprise*.

Uhura.

GET THE GIRL TO CHECK!

Fifteen Minutes in Space

In early 1961, President John F. Kennedy became the new President of the United States of America. With him came a new feeling of hope and excitement. President Kennedy was eager to get men into space. But on 12 April 1961, with a confident "Let's go!", Yuri Gagarin, a Soviet cosmonaut, as they called astronauts, blasted off to become the first man in space and – after 108 minutes of flight – the first man to orbit Earth. Despite the hard work of Katherine and everyone else at NASA, the USA was still in second place.

It was a disappointment for everyone at NASA, but it only made them more determined to make a success of the Mercury programme. Alan Shepard was picked to be the test subject for Katherine's equations: the first American in space. He named the capsule he would be travelling in *Freedom 7*.

J.F.K.

The launch was going to be televised, so millions of Americans could see exactly what was going on. One thing they fortunately did not see was what happened when Shepard needed to urinate. Apparently no one had planned for this, because he was already in his spacesuit and in the capsule.

There was no opportunity for him to leave the spacecraft and he very sensibly didn't want to spend all his time as the first American in space being desperate for a wee – so poor Shepard had to wee in his suit! There was no way of taking the urine out of the spacesuit, either. The result was damp, but luckily soon dried out. NASA learned a lesson from this. Later spacesuits would have systems built in to take away human waste. Being the first was a tough job!

WHAT'S SPACE EVER DONE FOR EARTH?

Many unexpected benefits have come about as a result of research into space travel. You might be the next person to discover something world-changing by accident! NASA's research has brought about innovations that have transformed our lives, including:

- Special cooling suits for people with burns injuries and multiple sclerosis
- Better breathing equipment for fire-fighters.
- Safer school buses.
- Special roofing material for football stadiums.
- Better GPS (global positioning satellites) that makes the maps on your phone work.
- Special methods for restoring priceless paintings.
- Special methods for reading ancient manuscripts buried by volcanoes.

The *Mercury-Redstone* rocket carrying Alan Shepard lifted off from Cape Canaveral, Florida, at 9:34 am on 5 May 1961. Once it had blasted through Earth's atmosphere, the rocket separated and fell back to Earth, landing safely away from people. The capsule, *Freedom 7*, reached a height of 187 km (116 miles). As planned, Shepard was able to control the capsule, which was something Yuri Gagarin had not been able to do. Shepard spent most of the flight observing the ground below and testing out the spacecraft's steering and handling, before returning to Earth. Buoyed up by its parachutes, the capsule landed in the sea 486 km (303 miles) from its launching point: right in the planned position for the navy ship to collect it. Alan Shepard had gone up an ordinary American and come down the first American in space – thanks to Katherine's equations.

Alan Shepard spent several minutes of his fifteen-and-a-half-minute flight in space. Compared to the amount of time Yuri Gagarin had been up there, it wasn't much. But it was a start. President John F. Kennedy gave Shepard a victory parade and announced that America's goal would now be to put a man on the Moon within ten years. It was an enormous challenge. Luckily, Katherine loved challenges.

John Glenn

If a journey of a thousand miles begins with a single step, a journey of 238,900 miles – the distance from the Earth to the Moon – has to begin with many, many carefully planned steps. The trajectories Katherine Johnson had calculated for Alan Shepard's flight were one of the most crucial first steps in a series of first steps, tests, and challenges in getting to the Moon. Each of these steps had everything riding on it.

One of the most important steps was to carry out an orbit of the Earth – ideally, more than one. For this mission, Katherine would not be carrying out calculations directly – she would be programming a computer to carry them out for her. In a way, the computer was doing the 'little stuff', while she did the thinking!

The man picked to be the first American to orbit the Earth was John Glenn, a test pilot. The mission would be dangerous, even for a man who was used to danger. He would be shot into the air on an Atlas rocket – a piece of machinery that had managed to blow up once in five test runs, and fail a second time. Meanwhile, the Russians placed yet another cosmonaut into space, and kept him in orbit for a full day. NASA was under great pressure but John Glenn kept calm and patient while NASA tested and re-tested the highly complex, delicate machinery that his life would be riding on. Then, three days before his launch, he asked for a safety test of his own.

By now, Katherine's job included programming electronic computers to do the calculations she used to do in her head. An IBM 7090 computer had calculated the orbital trajectory for John Glenn's mission: the path he would be sent on when he left Earth. However, the astronauts had never been one hundred per cent confident in the new-fangled electronic computers. Those electronic computers had been known to make mistakes. They had been known to break down. No astronaut, no matter how courageous, wanted to feel that a digit out of place could lead to them missing their re-entry by miles and heading out, like a ship completely off-course, into deep space with no way back. After all, electronic computers didn't understand how important human life was.

John Glenn sent a message to the engineers. "Get the girl to check the numbers," he asked. He would have met Katherine while training at Langley, although he had no way of knowing who exactly would run the check. The message was passed back to Katherine. America's space hero wanted Katherine Johnson's word that his flight was safe to take.

Katherine checked the numbers. She re-did all the complex calculations that the IBM computer had done. It took her over twenty-four hours, but she got back to John Glenn confirming that the numbers were right. On 20 February 1962, placing his faith in the calculations of the girl from White Sulphur Springs who'd had to move over a hundred miles just to find a school that would accept her, John Glenn launched into space in a bid to become the first American to orbit Earth.

FAMOUS FIRSTS IN SPACE

1961: Yuri Gagarin is the first man in space.

1963: Valentina Tereshkova is the first woman in space.

1969: Neil Armstrong and Buzz Aldrin are the first men on the Moon.

1983: Sally Ride is the first American woman in space.

1983: Guion S. Bluford Jr is the first black American man in space.

1992: Mae Jemison is the first black American woman in space.

The launch had been delayed several times, partly to make sure that the weather was clear enough that it could be filmed. Katherine, watching on television, could follow her equations as they took practical shape and form before her eyes.

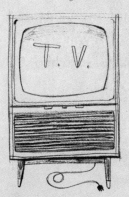

The Atlas rocket blasted off and swiftly reached Max Q, the technical name for the point at which the capsule was under the most strain from the forces trying to hold it back on Earth. If it had not been built well enough, it would simply explode. Speaking over the communication system, Glenn reported that it felt "bumpy" but soon it was clear that the capsule had survived. The booster rockets detached and the capsule continued into orbit.

Although the mission had been carefully and painstakingly planned out on the ground, it was impossible to prepare for everything that would happen during the actual flight. Every mission threw up some new detail that could change everything, perhaps catastrophically.

One of the most important factors was how well the capsule had been launched. Like a ski jumper, or a gymnast aiming to do mid-air somersaults, how you performed in the air depended on how well you started out. Launch well, and you gave yourself enough time to do several somersaults. Launch badly, and you would not have the time to turn even one. The orbits around Earth were like a gymnast's somersaults before gravity finally snatched them back.

A Circle Around the World

• •

Back on Earth the computers observed the trajectory that the rocket had launched the capsule into. It turned out that it was close to perfect: Glenn looked to be able to orbit the Earth at least seven times: a seven-somersault dive into star-studded sea. The number of orbits mattered, as that meant more time for Glenn to do experiments and conduct important research about travelling in space. During his fifteen minutes as a human cannon ball, Alan Shepard had not had time to do much more than try out the steering and look through a periscope – as his craft had no window. But John Glenn had nearly five hours in space. He had to observe as much as possible, confirm theories made on the ground and make a note of anything new of scientific interest. Given how little direct observation of space there had been so far, there were plenty of things to note down! He also had to control the capsule itself, turning it left and right and rolling it forwards and backwards. This proved difficult, but getting this right was crucial, as the capsule would need to be in the correct position at the correct time for the rockets to push him back to Earth. Then, of course, he had to deal with being in space: the acceleration, the g-forces and the lack of gravity. He also had to keep an eye out for any problems that cropped up, because not even Katherine Johnson could plan for all the things that could go wrong on this deep dive into space.

The spacecraft made three orbits of Earth, sending back data to the people and the electronic computers on the planet below. There were a few problems, for instance, Glenn's suit overheated, but when he tried cooling it off, this caused problems with the cabin temperature. He spent the flight trying to keep the two things in balance. But the most nail-biting moment came as the capsule headed down again. Katherine's equations had needed to account for the sheer difficulty of re-entering the atmosphere and surviving. The capsule had to come down at just the right angle and speed, or it would overheat and burn up. To protect the capsule and the astronaut, a heat shield had been added.

Now, the data coming back from the capsule seemed to show that that the heat shield was loose. It was only being held on by the retrorockets, but they were supposed to be jettisoned as Glenn came back down to earth.

Speaking over the communicator, NASA recommended that Glenn did not jettison the rockets. Anything out of the ordinary, like this message, was bound to ring alarm bells with the astronauts.

"What is the reason for this? Do you have any reason?" Glenn demanded.

"Not at this moment," replied the men on the ground.

Glenn quickly figured out there was a problem that they did not want to worry him with, but there was nothing he could do about it. He decided to trust the people on the ground. As he came down through the atmosphere at more than 27,400 km (17,000 miles) per hour there was radio blackout, meaning that he and mission control could not communicate with each other. Everyone could only hope and pray that the rockets would hold the heat shield on.

They did. From Glenn's point of view, it looked as if he was in a fireball as the rockets burned up and broke into bits, but the heat shield hung on. Then the capsule was through the atmosphere's barrier, but now it swayed back and forth, like a falling leaf, and still smotheringly hot inside. Just as Glenn was wondering if the parachutes that were supposed to deploy had failed, they opened. Freedom 7 splashed down safe and sound, just forty miles away from the planned position where a navy ship was waiting to pick him up. He had come home safely – thanks to Katherine's precise, accurate calculations.

Forty miles off course wasn't bad given what a complicated, difficult mission had just been accomplished. The total distance travelled had been approximately 105,000 km (65,763 miles), in just under five hours, orbiting Earth only three times out of the possible seven. Yet it also showed how the tiniest detail could change things. The forty-mile difference between the predicted landing site and the actual splashdown location had come about because the calculations for re-entry hadn't considered the loss of weight caused by the things on-board that had been used during the flight. That oversight was the kind of thing that could flip a mission from a glorious triumph into a tragic failure.

It was an incredible success, for everyone at NASA, and for the USA. John F. Kennedy shook John Glenn's hand and later declared to a delighted crowd,

"WE CHOOSE TO GO TO THE MOON IN THIS DECADE AND DO THE OTHER THINGS, NOT BECAUSE THEY ARE EASY,

BUT BECAUSE THEY ARE HARD... BECAUSE THAT CHALLENGE IS ONE THAT WE ARE WILLING TO ACCEPT, ONE WE ARE UNWILLING TO POSTPONE, AND ONE WHICH WE INTEND TO WIN."

The Face of Progress

The success of John Glenn's mission and the publicity around it changed Katherine's life in a way she could never have imagined when she first took up the job in the West Area Computing Unit. People started to want to know about her. They were intrigued and fascinated. Who was this woman who had plotted the mathematical course of America's greatest triumph to date? Black-owned newspapers like the *Pittsburgh Courier*, who were always keen to celebrate black Americans succeeding against all the odds, ran interviews with her. Katherine took the attention with characteristic modesty. The way she saw it, she had just been doing her job.

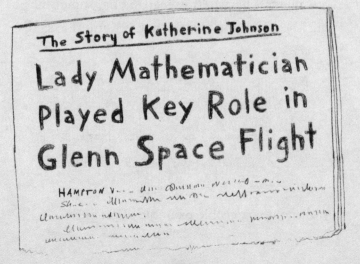

The Story of Katherine Johnson

Lady Mathematician Played Key Role in Glenn Space Flight

But the newspaper articles were important. Most coverage of the American space programme showed white men at the helm and white men on the ground. Meanwhile, the black employees of NASA, much less the black female employees, did not get any of the attention. Because of articles like the one in the *Pittsburgh Courier*, all across the USA, black families opened their newspapers to see the potential of what a black woman could achieve. They might have looked in the mirror, or looked at their sisters, daughters and mothers, and thought, "Well, if Katherine Johnson can do it, why can't I?" And white families, too, would have learned that when they saw a black woman, she could as easily be a research mathematician as a maid. The world was changing, sometimes quickly, sometimes slowly, but as Katherine said,

"YOU HAVE TO EXPECT PROGRESS TO BE MADE."

And she was a visible example of progress.

THREE DISASTERS

Death in Dallas

It was not even a hundred years since the first aeroplanes had taken to the skies, and now America was planning to send men to the Moon. The thought must have taken Katherine's breath away. Like a pilot with the throttle on full, humans were charging through change so fast that the world seemed to be a blur outside. And yet other things seemed to stay still, or have the brakes on, almost lurching backwards by comparison.

President John F. Kennedy was very supportive of NASA's space programme, and the plans to land man on the Moon. He was also supportive of equal rights. In a speech in 1963, Kennedy said, "This nation was founded by men of many nations and backgrounds. It was founded on the principle that all men are created equal, and that the rights of every man are diminished when the rights of one man are threatened."

John F. Kennedy proposed new laws that banned segregation and outlawed discrimination based on race, religion or nationality in all public places. States would no longer be able to make their own rules. To many, the young President symbolized America's hopes and dreams of progress. But later the same year, in November 1963, as he was being driven through Dallas, Texas, in an open-topped car, he was shot dead by a gunman.

Americans were stunned and horrified by the assassination. Vice President Lyndon Baines Johnson was quickly sworn in as the new President, and the alleged gunman, Lee Harvey Oswald, was himself shot and killed by a member of the public while being escorted between prisons. All of it was caught on live television, America's unforgiving magic mirror.

At NASA, the assassination was felt as keenly as anywhere else. President Kennedy had been a cheerleader for space; he had proposed challenges that at first seemed impossible, but later gave

NASA's employees confidence in their abilities. The shock hardened into determination. Gene Krantz, flight director of mission control, later said that they felt they were going to the Moon for President Kennedy. They were on a crusade now to make the President's dreams come true. Project Mercury was followed by Project Gemini, which aimed to develop further techniques that would make a lunar landing possible. Gemini was followed by the Apollo programme, which was going to take men to the Moon, by the end of the decade – no matter what the cost. Katherine was as determined as anyone to make it work.

It was a thrilling challenge. Before, when she calculated the trajectories for Alan Shepherd and John Glenn, she had only had to consider the forces acting on the Earth, and how to escape and re-enter their power safely. Now, working on the Apollo missions, she not only had to include the Earth in her calculations, but also the forces acting on the Moon – where no one had ever been before. But before she could calculate a pathway, NASA had to design the spacecraft that was capable of getting to the Moon.

We Choose to Go to the Moon...
But How?

NASA had a couple of ideas about how to achieve a lunar landing. One idea was direct ascent. An incredibly powerful rocket would simply push a spacecraft to the Moon, without entering lunar orbit. Unfortunately, that kind of powerful rocket didn't exist. The other idea was more complicated, and more risky. It was called lunar orbit rendezvous. In this scenario, a rocket would carry a two-part system into space. There would be a command module and a lunar module. On reaching the Moon's orbit, the lunar module

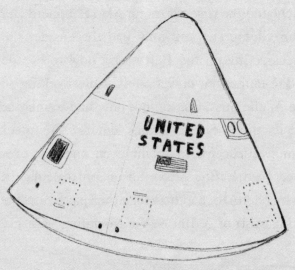

would detach from the command module. At least one astronaut would stay behind in the command module, orbiting the Moon, while others went down to the surface of the Moon in the lunar module. Then they would have to take off from the Moon again, leaving part of the module behind, and reattach to the command module, before returning to Earth.

An upside of lunar orbit rendezvous, compared to direct ascent, was that little rocket fuel was needed to move around in space, or to escape the Moon's weak gravity. The downside was a classic problem for engineers: it was more complicated. There were more moving parts and more connections. That meant there was much more that could go wrong. That was the engineering challenge.

Katherine, however, had a different challenge – a mathematical one. The trajectories she had calculated so far had explained how to send a manned spacecraft beyond Earth's atmosphere, enter into Earth's orbit and return through the atmosphere to a pre-determined spot without being destroyed. But that was dealing with just one planet, one object in space. Each body in space – planet, moon or star – had its own conditions. She now had to account for the very different conditions on the Moon. Her calculations would have to account for its gravity, its rotation around its own axis and its revolution around the Earth. It would be a little like launching from a football being kicked through the air and attempting to land on a baseball flying through the air in a different stadium. And then of course, everything had to be run in reverse. She'd have to calculate how to get the astronauts off the Moon, and back to Earth.

When early sailors set out into the open oceans, they took a risk. Some believed that the Earth was flat, and that if they went too far, they would fall off the edge. Even when they knew the Earth was round, the seas were still full of danger. Travelling in Earth's orbit was a bit like sailing in the shallows, around familiar coasts whose tides you knew. Going to the Moon was like setting off to find a new continent. However, mathematics and astronomy meant it was possible to predict the conditions in space, and to work out what was needed in order to send astronauts safely to the Moon and back. The football and the baseball had both been thrown many times over and over again, and always followed the same path. One strand of Katherine's research was accurately calculating how to move from the football to the baseball and back again, safely.

We Choose to Go to the Moon... No Matter What the Cost?

Katherine's other strand of research was running "what if?" calculations. What if this goes wrong? What if that breaks down? What should the astronauts do then? Up there, isolated in a bubble in the emptiness of space, the astronauts were so alone. As pilots, they didn't understand everything about the machine that was keeping them alive – how could they? The missions into space were becoming so technical that it was impossible for any single person to understand everything about them. The success of a mission to the Moon would always have to be a team effort, with thousands of people making up the team. There had to be a procedure, a protocol, for every scenario, no matter how unlikely. No one at mission control wanted that sinking, helpless feeling that came from being thousands of miles from brave people who depended on you, who were asking, "What do we do now?", and not having a reply for them. Mission control had come up with a solution when John Glenn's heat shield was thought to have failed, but the Apollo missions were even more complicated. Everything had to be thought through by the people on the ground, like Katherine.

To make it even more nerve-wracking, the whole journey would take place in front of witnesses, because right from the start television was part of the plan. The astronauts flying to the Moon would have a large part of their journey broadcast on live television. If something went wrong – an error in Katherine's calculations for example – there would be no way of hiding it. Apollo would consist of many missions, each designed to test out a different step in the process of getting men to the Moon. Every step had to be mastered, as if they were learning a dance routine, before putting it all together for the big show – the live performance when everything had to go perfectly. The difference was that in a dance show, no one was risking their life.

The First Apollo Mission

In 1967, *Apollo 1* was almost ready to go. It was to be the first mission of the Apollo project that would have a crew on board. The three astronauts – Gus Grissom, Ed White and Roger Chaffee – were full of excitement and anticipation. Gus Grissom told the nation that he expected to stay in orbit for fourteen days, and NASA announced that there would be a television camera on board for live broadcasts during the flight.

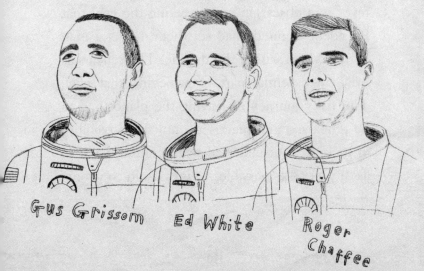

Gus Grissom   Ed White   Roger Chaffee

On 27 January 1967, the three astronauts were in the spacecraft for a rehearsal of the launch, strapped in and wearing their spacesuits. It had been a long day, fraught with problems, and everyone was getting tired and irritable.

"How are we going to get to the Moon if we can't talk between three buildings?" said one of the astronauts when the communication system broke down yet again.

Everyone at NASA was working long hours at this point, including Katherine, who was focused not just on charts and trajectories, but also on having an answer for every problem: drawing up back-up procedures so that the astronauts and mission control would never be without a plan. The flight director would later describe it as "goal fever": an obsession with meeting the goal that President Kennedy had set them, to get a man on the Moon within the decade. The rehearsals were an essential part of achieving that goal. The risky journey of leaving the planet had to be rehearsed and practised until the possibility of making a mistake had been ground down to as tiny a risk as possible. Things could go wrong, everyone knew that. Yet nobody was expecting things to go wrong as suddenly, unexpectedly and as terribly as they did aboard *Apollo 1.*

There were thirty miles of electrical wire in the spacecraft. Somewhere in those thirty miles, during that rehearsal, an electrical fire broke out. The fire spread through the pure oxygen in the cabin. The door was securely fastened with many latches, and the spacecraft was at a different pressure than the air outside. As a result, the astronauts couldn't open the door fast enough to escape. Nor could the people outside who were frantically trying to help them get out. The three astronauts died.

Like everyone at NASA, Katherine was devastated. These were not faceless heroes, they were men who had been with NASA for years, the people at the receiving end of her mathematical skills. It was a reminder of how much was at stake, and it was a dreadful beginning to the Apollo project.

For everyone at NASA, it was a brutal wake-up call. The men had not even been in space. The danger had not come from outside, but from inside. Investigations showed that small details had been overlooked, which had led to the astronauts' deaths. "We were the cause," flight director Gene Kranz told his team. "Nothing we did had a shelf-life. From now on we will be tough and competent." This, he told the intently listening NASA staff, was the price of admission to NASA, so that what happened to Gus Grissom, Ed White and Roger Chaffee would never, ever be forgotten.

The Murder of Martin Luther King

Throughout the 1950s and 1960s, television opened Americans' eyes to what other Americans thought and believed. Like rockets and spacecraft, it was a technology that was encouraging change in society, too. The young, charismatic preacher, Martin Luther King Jr, delivered speeches that captivated and inspired the world – and that were seen by many more people because of television. In 1963 he told a rapt crowd,

"I HAVE A DREAM THAT MY FOUR LITTLE CHILDREN WILL ONE DAY LIVE IN A NATION WHERE THEY WILL NOT BE JUDGED BY THE COLOUR OF THEIR SKIN, BUT THE CONTENT OF THEIR CHARACTER."

In 1964, President Lyndon B. Johnson signed the Civil Rights Act that President Kennedy had outlined. To many people, it was a step forward, an assertion that progress and change for the better would not be stopped by violence. Many Americans still resented change, but slowly, the push forward was overcoming the resistance, like a rocket forcing its way through the atmosphere, into the great possibilities of space.

Then on 4 April 1968, another American hero was shot dead. Martin Luther King Jr was assassinated. For black Americans, and for many white people too, it was a tragedy and a disaster. It was a horrible reminder that some people would do anything to stop progress. Yet even the tragedy of Martin Luther King Jr's murder could not turn back the changes of the Civil Rights Act. Progress had already happened. It was possible for someone like Katherine, born in 1918, to look around and see real change. Martin Luther King Jr had been a big fan of *Star Trek* and of the character Uhura, played by Nichelle Nichols, a black American actress. He had told Nichelle Nichols that because of her role,

"… on television, we will be seen as we should be seen every day, as intelligent, quality, beautiful people … who can go into space, who can be lawyers and teachers, who can be professors." Katherine might have added, "and who can be research mathematicians at NASA." The death of Martin Luther King Jr was a tragedy, but it did not mean giving up. Katherine was going to be one of the people who put men on the Moon. After all, she had survived tragedy and prejudice to find new happiness and make a success of bringing up her three daughters. How much harder could putting a man on the Moon be?

Earth, Rising

However, before NASA could put men on the Moon, they had to send them into lunar orbit. The journey of thousands of miles had to be done in steps and stages, trying out each stage and testing it for risk and danger, before putting them all together for the big show. Before setting foot on the Moon, astronauts would have to leave

Earth on a trajectory calculated to take them out of orbit and across hundreds of thousands of miles of space, further from Earth than any other living being had ever gone before. They would have to fire rockets, sending spacecraft to intercept the Moon's orbit and be pulled into its embrace, becoming its satellite. Those rockets had to be fired at precisely the right moment – too early or too late, too powerful or too weak, and the spacecraft would end up crashing into the Moon, or spinning off, helplessly, into deep space. Though it had never been tried before, Katherine had confidence that the rules of mathematics held across the universe. She just had to be right, and being right meant being precise and careful – all the time and every time.

On 21 December 1968, *Apollo 8* astronauts Frank Borman, Jim Lovell and William Anders became the first humans to leave Earth's orbit and make the 384,400 km (238,855 miles) journey to the Moon. For most of the mission, the spacecraft was controlled from Earth, based on trajectories that Katherine had calculated. It took them nearly three days to reach lunar orbit.

As planned, they sent live television and radio broadcasts back to Earth, and tried to describe what they were seeing.

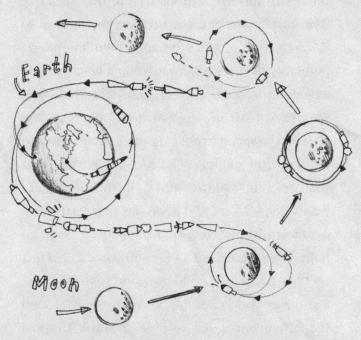

The numbers didn't fail them. What Katherine had always liked about maths was that you could be either right or wrong, so she had simply made sure she was always right. The Moon was far away, but with maths you could go anywhere. She could make a calculation and know that it was correct, even though the objects she was analyzing were thousands of miles away.

But being so far from Earth posed some problems for the astronauts aboard *Apollo 8*. The three men became the first humans to go through the Van Allen radiation belt. They wore detectors to check their radiation levels – which, as predicted, were not dangerous because of the speed at which they passed through the belt. The parts of the spacecraft facing the Sun were heated to over 200 degrees Celsius, while the parts that were in shadow could drop to 100 degrees below zero. To try and keep the spacecraft from overheating, the crew had to rotate it once an hour. With typical NASA humour, they called this the "barbecue roll". This was the first time that astronauts had been able to move freely around the cabin, but it led to illness: Frank Borman developed vomiting and diarrhoea, a condition later named space adaptation syndrome. Being the first to do anything was hard, as Alan Shepard had found out, and not always as glamorous as the people on Earth might believe. But as the three men orbited the Moon ten times between

Christmas Eve and Christmas Day 1968, they had no regrets at all. They took photographs which caused a sensation – above all, the image of Earth appearing over the horizon of the Moon, which became known as Earthrise.

It was the first time that humans had ever seen their planet as a whole, from the outside. Like a fragile, beautiful soap bubble, it hovered, isolated in the endless darkness of space. Nowadays, that image is everywhere, but to those who were the first generation to see it, it was breathtaking to realize that everyone they knew and cared about was on that one, shimmering sphere in space. Many people had always said that the Earth was a whole, each part of it linked, but to see it in such a powerful image made that truth somehow more real to everyone. NASA had not planned it, nor had they expected it, but the voyage of *Apollo 8* changed how people thought about their planet and their existence.

"We set out to explore the Moon and instead discovered the Earth," said William Anders, fifty years after taking the photograph. Science could discover new facts, but it could also change people's hearts and minds: out of the race to conquer space came an unexpected benefit, a new respect and awe for Earth, and a new desire to protect the fragile environment. Nationality, race and colour seemed like silly, trivial ideas. Silently, the image brought home to everyone who saw it the fact that the Earth – and all the people on it, regardless of skin colour – was one, perfect whole. Martin Luther King Jr might have been murdered, but the Earth itself seemed to be repeating his words: wasn't it unthinkable, given how linked all life on Earth was, to judge people on anything other than the content of their characters?

WHY GO TO THE MOON?

"America has reached out to the stars but not reached out to her starving poor": Rev Ralph D. Abernathy, civil rights leader.

Not everyone thought that it was right to spend billions of dollars on sending a few people to the Moon, when so many people in America were living in poverty. Gil Scott-Heron, a well-known poet, musician and writer, expressed this sense of unfairness in a poem called "Whitey on the Moon". Going to the Moon was seen as a luxury for white people, not something that included black Americans.

A black-owned newspaper, *the Los Angeles Sentinel*, wrote furiously in an article published after the Moon landings, that the government was prepared to: "contaminate the Moon and its sterility for the sake of 'progress' and spend billions of dollars in the process, while people are hungry, ill-clothed, poorly educated (if at all)."

Many black Americans were disgusted by the government's obsession with the Moon and rivalry with the Soviet Union, and its failure to protect its own poorest citizens.

At the launch of *Apollo 14*, 200 people protested

against what one civil rights leader, Hosea Williams, described as "our nation's inability to choose humane priorities." It was not just black people who felt the Moon landings were a waste of money – throughout the 1960s, most Americans thought that the space programme was not worth it. One sociologist, Amitai Etzioni, wrote that: "by focusing on the Moon we delay facing ourselves, as Americans and as citizens of the earth."

What do you think? Is space travel worth the money that is spent on it?

THE MOON WILL BE THERE WHEN YOU GET THERE

Rendezvous

During the 1960s, Katherine worked with a team of engineers after Ted Skopinski, including John Mayer, Alton Mayo, Al Hamer and Carl Huss. She did not simply carry out instructions, but pushed the engineers she was working with to do better and to think harder. She was even able to suggest alternative approaches when the engineers got stuck. She co-authored four reports during the 1960s, some mathematical, others establishing protocol for everything that could go wrong. What if, for example, the automatic guidance system failed between Earth and the Moon? How would the astronauts know where they were and how to get home? In 1967, together with Al Hamer, Katherine wrote a report that showed the astronauts how to use geometry to work out where they were from the stars that they could see, and how to use maths to calculate the trajectory they would need to take to get home. No one wanted to have to use the procedure, but it was in place to save lives in an emergency. But when Katherine was asked in a later interview which work she was proudest of, she answered, "Working on the lunar rendezvous."

Rendezvous was absolutely essential to the success of *Apollo 11*'s 1969 mission to land on the Moon. With the disaster of *Apollo 1* still scarring their memories – mission control would later say that there was a NASA "before the fire" and a NASA "after the fire" – everyone was on high alert for all the many things that could possibly go wrong. The most likely place for anything to go wrong was during rendezvous, because nothing like this had been attempted before. The Soviets had not done it either.

Most of the flight would be controlled and programmed from Earth. That meant that everyone on Earth who was responsible for it was manoeuvring not just a piece of complex engineering, but also three lives: those of Neil

Armstrong, Buzz Aldrin and Michael Collins. There were three possible outcomes: landing, aborting or crashing. Landing would mean success. Aborting would mean failure. Crashing would mean disaster. If *Apollo 11* crashed, it would almost certainly kill the men aboard. Crucial decisions would have to be made by the flight controllers during the mission, each man responsible for making calls that could lead to success, failure or death. It was crucial that the information they were given was correct and reliable. That was where Katherine came in. She calculated the pathways that the lunar module would have to take to rendezvous with the command module.

The Eagle Lands

Katherine Johnson was not in mission control when Eagle landed, she was at a sorority reunion in the Poconos mountains, watching the Moon landing on television. She had more insight than most people into the preparation that lay

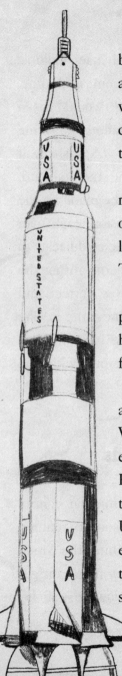

behind this moment. Yet now, all she could do was watch along with the rest of the world as the countdown began – and hope that everything went to plan.

"3, 2, 1, 0 … All engines running. Lift off! We have a lift off … 32 minutes past the hour, lift off on *Apollo 11*. Tower clear." The first challenge was a success.

The rocket, *Saturn V*, the most powerful rocket in existence, had successfully broken free from the Earth.

Saturn V was massive, complex, and weighed six million pounds. With the exception of a nuclear explosion, the noise that roared in Katherine's ears as it lifted off was the loudest man-made noise ever. Unseen by the viewers, complex engineering beneath it deflected the energy the rocket produced so that it didn't burn itself up

– another part of the essential background work it had taken to get to this moment.

Katherine continued to watch, as *Saturn V* carried the spacecraft up through the atmosphere. As planned, it detached from the spacecraft once it had lifted it free of the atmosphere. The enormous rocket, its job done, fell away and left the much smaller spacecraft to carry on through space. That stage was called the trans-lunar injection.

Apollo 11 didn't need much fuel on the way to the Moon – that was "cruise mode", and it was the longest part of the journey. Because nothing stood in the way of the spacecraft, it could fly for miles with very little effort. The next difficult bit came after seventy-five hours and fifty minutes, when the astronauts began to move the spacecraft into the orbit of the Moon. That stage was called lunar orbit insertion. But Katherine could not watch it happen, and nor could anyone on Earth. Lunar Orbit insertion had to happen – if it was successful – on the far side of the Moon that is never visible from Earth, and where the Moon's body cut off all communication with Earth. Until the spacecraft emerged, no one on Earth would know if the action had been successful.

If it wasn't successful, the men could crash into the surface of the Moon, or the spacecraft could go spinning off into deep space, lost forever. The people on Earth held their breath.

Lunar orbit insertion was a success. The spacecraft was now orbiting the Moon.

Now came the tense moments leading up to the actual landing on the Moon. Following plans made on Earth long before, the lunar module detached from the command module and the two astronauts inside – Neil Armstrong and Buzz Aldrin – would guide it down to the Moon.

The third man, Michael Collins, remained in orbit. As the others explored the Moon, his job was to remain piloting the command module while staying in touch both with the astronauts on the surface of the Moon, and mission control on Earth.

The Sea of Tranquillity

It was only when they got to the point of landing on the Moon that the power of mathematics ran out for the astronauts. The planned landing site was in the Sea of Tranquillity, a large crater, named in 1651 by Italian astronomers who thought that the dark areas on the Moon might be seas. *Apollo 11* descended to the surface of the Moon, but to the people at flight control, it seemed they were going much too fast. Katherine must have held her breath at this moment, hoping that everything would not go wrong.

At mission control, the flight controllers had to decide whether to abort the mission to save the crew from a crash. They had only seconds to make the decision. They held their nerve – and the descent stabilized. But then Neil and Buzz got a glimpse of the surface they were heading for. No one had seen the surface of the Moon this close up before, so it was not possible to plan in detail for this moment. It turned out that the Moon was covered in boulders, some as big as houses. It was going to be nearly impossible to land safely.

With the fuel running low, Neil Armstrong had to fly the lunar module, looking for a safe place to land among the boulders. Flight control could only watch as the instruments told them that there were sixty, then thirty, seconds left before the lunar module ran out of fuel and crashed. With fifteen seconds left, they heard Neil Armstrong speak the words: "Tranquility Base here ... the Eagle has landed."

Across the world, people saw a group of white men, with the same short haircuts, the same width of tie and the same style shirts – like a uniform – celebrating in the mission control centres. Viewers would have unconsciously concluded that this was the face of space – white and male. But Katherine had been working sixteen-hour days to get men to the Moon, too. Television did not always show the whole truth.

But as Martin Luther King Jr had told Nichelle Nichols, it could show the truth, and it could inspire. Of the millions of people watching the Moon landings that day, one of them was a little girl in Chicago called Mae Jemison. It didn't escape her notice that all the men at NASA were, well, men. "Why are there no women astronauts?" she wondered.

Why couldn't she be an astronaut too?

Mae Jemison did not know Katherine, and Katherine did not know her, but they had more in common than they might have imagined: great intelligence and a passion for space.

Like stars in a constellation joining up to make a picture in the night sky, Mae, Katherine and the many others like them came together to make a picture of a different face of space, a face that could be black and female.

MAE JEMISON

- Mae Jemison was born in Alabama in 1956.
- In kindergarten, she told her teacher that she wanted to be a scientist. "Don't you mean a nurse?" replied the teacher. Mae did not! She knew exactly what she wanted to be. Watching the Moon landings in 1969, she questioned why there were no women astronauts.

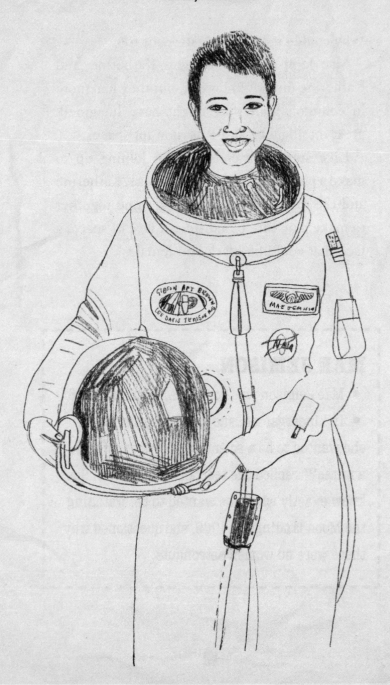

- Mae Jemison started studying at Stanford University at age 16 and graduated with a degree in chemical engineering.

- She was also a talented dancer but chose to go to medical school at Cornell University. She worked as a doctor, in the USA and abroad, saving lives – but she always wanted to go into space.

- After Sally Ride became the first American woman in space, Mae decided that she might have a chance of getting into the astronaut programme, so she applied – and was selected.

- She became the first black American woman to go into space.

- In 1993, she resigned as an astronaut in order to found her own company, developing science and technology for use in everyday life.

- She has received numerous awards and honours for her many achievements in science.

"THE BEST WAY TO MAKE DREAMS COME TRUE IS TO WAKE UP."

And Back Again

On the Moon, Neil Armstrong and Buzz Aldrin had plenty to do. This was an incredible chance for science, and there were plenty of tasks planned for them to carry out. They collected samples of rocks and dust from the Moon. These would help scientists learn about the Moon, but also about the Earth and about outerspace.

After twenty-one and a half hours, the

moment had come for the two men to leave. They returned to the lunar module. Part of that had been designed to be able to lift off from the Moon. This was called the lunar ascender. The rest of it remained on the Moon.

Katherine had a special reason to pay close attention to the next stage, which was called lunar orbit rendezvous – she had worked on the mathematics behind it. The lunar ascender rose up from the Moon, to meet and join on to, the command module above. It was something that had never been attempted before. The two spacecrafts needed to connect and allow the astronauts to safely move from one to the other without the risk of being sucked out into the vacuum of space. But, as Katherine well knew, it wasn't as simple as floating up and meeting a hovering object. Orbit was fast. Both of the modules were going faster than a bullet fired from a gun. To get them next to each other and connect them without crashing them was the tricky part. It was like trying to thread a needle that was on a different planet.

It was a nail-biting moment for everyone

watching from Earth. But the two modules lined up exactly. Lunar orbit rendezvous went without a hitch. Katherine could breathe a sigh of relief. Her calculations had worked perfectly.

After a flight of 195 hours, 18 minutes, 35 seconds, *Apollo 11* and the three astronauts splashed down safely in the Pacific Ocean. The Moon landing was a complete success – and Katherine, along with the rest of NASA, could celebrate the triumph for which they had worked so hard.

What If?

Apollo 11 was an enormous success, a world-changing first. Yet the next Apollo missions demonstrated that the unexpected could still go wrong, and that it took a team on the ground to keep the men on the Moon. Just after launch, *Apollo 12* was struck by lightning, blowing out all the electrics in the command module. One flight controller, John Aaron, remembered a simulation he had seen a year before in training that looked a lot like the disaster unfolding before them. "Try switching SCE to Aux," he told them. Even the flight director had no idea what he was talking about, but he passed the message on. The astronauts did it – and luckily it worked! 'Tough and competent', Gene Kranz had said after the disaster of *Apollo 1*: now everyone at NASA made it their business to have a solution in a crisis. The second mission to send men to the Moon was a success. When things went wrong in space travel, it was usually a problem with the physical materials, rather than the mathematics. The protocols for the "what if?" scenarios that Katherine helped develop, saved lives.

*

By 1970, broadcasting from space had become routine. NASA could show people that America was leading in space, live. In 1970, *Apollo 13* had lifted off without problems and was two days into its journey to the Moon. The crew had just completed forty-nine minutes of live broadcasting to Earth, showing their viewers how they lived and worked in zero gravity. Viewers saw them floating around, upside down, talking calmly and even sounding a little bored. It was a far cry from the early missions, where Alan Shepard and John Glenn had been strapped in, unable to move, like human cannonballs fired helplessly through the sky. This was more like really living in space: sleeping, eating and having a conversation just as they did on *Star Trek*. Viewers on Earth could imagine themselves, one day, doing something similar. Then, just nine minutes after the end of the broadcast, one oxygen tank blew up, and the second one failed.

"HOUSTON, WE'VE HAD A PROBLEM HERE,"

announced the astronauts. They did not yet know about the oxygen leak, but they discovered it soon enough when they looked out of the window of the capsule and saw a stream of gas blowing out into space. That was their oxygen, the gas they needed to keep them alive. Because of the explosion, the power also went down, causing the temperature to drop. They were 321,900 km (200,000 miles) from Earth in an environment that was completely hostile to human life, and their life support system, their spacecraft, was failing fast.

NASA's Greatest Moment?

NASA took control from the ground. The first thing they did was to officially abort the mission: these men would not be landing on the Moon. They would be lucky to even land back on Earth. The next thing was to move the astronauts out of the command module, which had lost power, into the lunar module. The first question was, could the lunar module, which was designed to keep two men alive for two days, keep three men alive for much longer? The second question was how were they going to get home? The booster rockets would have to be fired in exactly the right way to send the spacecraft on the right trajectory towards Earth.

Over the next couple of days, NASA worked frantically to find ways to keep the crew alive and get them back down to Earth safely. The astronauts would have to get back into the command module at the last moment and switch the power back on, to try to conserve the emergency back-up battery power. That meant getting back into the area of the spacecraft that had been exposed to the freezing temperatures of space. Worse still, their water supply was running out. Not only did the astronauts need drinking water to stay alive, but water was also vital for keeping the mechanisms from over-heating. The astronauts cut down the water they consumed. Carbon monoxide was building up from the astronauts' breath, and systems had to be improvised to filter it out of the air. Navigation was difficult because debris flying past the window made it impossible to spot the stars.

At the last moment, the astronauts transferred back into the command module and switched the power back on. The module was covered in condensation droplets, clammy and cold, and as they went through the atmosphere, Commander Lovell recalled that "it rained in the command module".

When *Apollo 13* splashed down in the Pacific Ocean, the mission might have been considered a failure because the spacecraft never reached the Moon. To NASA, despite the disappointment, it was a success – because against all the odds they had got the astronauts back home safely.

Katherine, too, had succeeded against all the odds. Her work at NASA had taken long hours out of her life, but with the help and support of her husband, family and friends, her children had grown up into intelligent and responsible young women. In a later interview Joylette Goble said that her mother taught her not to accept failure, to help others wherever possible, and to believe that: "If there is a job to be done, you can do it and do it until you finish." Katherine Goble Moore said that she would "always be grateful" for her mother. To her daughters, Katherine Johnson was a role model – all three graduated from Hampton University, and chose to follow their mother into careers involving teaching, maths and science.

MORE MOON FACTS

• The temperature on the Moon ranges from 120 degrees Celsius (hotter than boiling water) to minus 170 degrees Celsius (colder than anywhere on Earth's surface).

• If you were on the Moon without your space suit, you would die in less than a minute.

LEGACY

A New Kind of Future

For the rest of her time working at NASA, Langley, Katherine continued to work on developing space travel. Her work didn't grab headlines, but it was quietly important, and as always, she "did her job correctly and well". It was that kind of dedication from the whole team, or family, at NASA, that made the headline-grabbing events possible.

Many people had dreamed that after men on the Moon would come permanent bases on the Moon, perhaps towns and cities. That was not what happened. Things on Earth changed. The Soviet Union collapsed, the Cold War came to an end, and with it, the Space Race. Almost as soon as NASA had put men on the Moon, it stopped putting men on the Moon. The last man to walk on the Moon was astronaut Eugene Cernan in

1972. No woman, and no black American, had the chance to get up there before the American Moon-landing programme was shelved.

Many people today wonder why the USA would give up on a programme that had been so successful, and which seemed to be the most exciting thing that humans could possibly be involved in. But the truth was that going into space cost a lot of money, and more and more people were asking to see it justified, with results that could be experienced on Earth. Instead of putting more men on the Moon, NASA began turning to new challenges. They set out to design a space shuttle – a reusable form of space transportation. It would be a kind of aeroplane that could launch like a rocket and then fly back down again to land on the ground, rather than splashing into the ocean. The space shuttle would fly up to a space station, called Skylab, a structure in low Earth orbit, to house astronauts who would engage in scientific study that would benefit Earth. Aboard a space station, astronauts could learn more about the Universe, but also explore science and technology that could be of use on Earth.

Katherine's new research was about how to make the structures that would be put into orbit around Earth safe, stable and strong.

SPACE STATIONS: BUILDING A HOME IN SPACE

Space stations are used to house astronauts for long periods of time. The first space stations were built and launched by the Soviet Union. The very first one was called Salyut 1, and it was launched in 1971. Until 1986, several Salyut space stations were in use. Like all space stations, they were built in space, not on Earth, and they did not return to Earth until they crashed out of orbit. They were not transportation, but homes and places for research, built with workshops, laboratories and with experiments running all the time.

The first space station launched by NASA was called Skylab. It was launched in 1973, but was damaged during the launch when part of it tore away. As a result, it was only occupied for 24 weeks, between 1973 and 1974. It fell out of orbit back to Earth in 1979, before it could be repaired enough to be reused. This was a disappointment to the astronauts who had hoped to go and work there. It also made the government think hard about how much money they spent on the space programme. Was it worth it, when an investment of so much money could so easily be destroyed?

Katherine also researched large antenna systems that could be placed into orbit around Earth, that would be used for, among other things, email systems and weather surveillance. Working on the space shuttle would have felt a little like déjà vu: the idea had developed from the X-15, a hypersonic aircraft that had been proposed at NACA in 1954. In some ways her area of expertise, the mathematics of flight, hadn't really changed. The politicians' priorities were different and the risks were always unpredictable, but Earth was Earth, gravity was gravity and sound was sound. The laws of mathematics and physics weren't going to change, but the ways in which mathematicians could apply them were infinitely interesting. And the natural next step, after the Moon, was the other planets. Perhaps one day, the laws would help people fly to other planets. But for now, the focus was to understand Earth.

SIMPLE AERODYNAMICS ACTIVITIES

Scrunch up a ball of paper and throw it across the room. (Don't use your mum's work!) How far and fast does it travel?

Now make a paper aeroplane.

How far and fast does it fly? Would you rather be travelling in the ball of paper, or the paper aeroplane?

The paper aeroplane travels faster and further because it has better aerodynamics. It is streamlined so that it has little resistance to the air. Modern aeroplanes have wings that change position after take-off, swinging back to make them more dart-shaped and provide less air resistance.

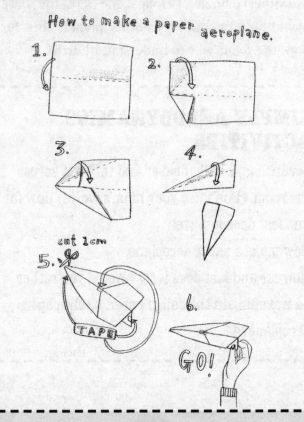

How to make a paper aeroplane.

1.

2.

3.

4.

5. cut 1cm

TAPE

6.

GO!

Where Next?

Travelling to Mars was suddenly looking more possible than it had ever looked before. To get there, you would use the laws of physics and mathematics once again, swinging the spacecraft around the Moon and then breaking it out of orbit at just the right moment, like a child on a playground roundabout, to launch on a trajectory towards Mars. Then, an orbital insertion would be used, accounting for the gravity, rotation and revolution of the red planet. Of course, Mars was just the start: all the other planets could be reached, the gas giants of Jupiter and Saturn, the distant outposts of Uranus and Neptune, in just the same way. And then this was only one solar system in the galaxy of stars, only one galaxy in a Universe of worlds...

Of course, things weren't that simple. NASA would have to build more spacecraft, and the fuel needed to reach these distant worlds would be incredibly expensive. But probes could be sent, flying out like little stones skipping over the sea. Telescopes could be mounted in space, like a giant pair of binoculars for the Earth to peer through to get a good look into the depths of space and the depths of time – because light came from long ago as well as far away. You could look back at the beginning of the Universe, if you wanted to. Now that people could get to the Moon, they could do anything.

In 1978, NASA Astronaut Group 8 recruited new astronauts, the first group to recruit women. This group was recruited, not to travel in spacecraft like the ones used on the Apollo programme, but to travel on the space shuttle programme. They would not be flying to the Moon but to a space station – although as it happened, Skylab fell to Earth in 1979, before they could reach it.

Out of thousands of applicants, only thirty-five were chosen for Astronaut Group 8. Two of the new recruits were Sally Ride and Guion S. Bluford. Sally Ride was a physicist and Guion Bluford was an officer in the United States Air Force. They would go on to achieve two significant firsts: in 1983, Sally Ride became the first American woman in space. A couple of months later, Guion Bluford became the first black American in space. It had taken decades, but a new normal had been established. Women like Katherine Johnson, by following their dreams and refusing to be discouraged from careers that seemed closed off to them due to racism, had slowly but steadily broken down the barriers of prejudice. Because Katherine had followed her dreams, other women could follow theirs.

*

1986 was another significant year in space. It was notable for a disaster that demonstrated that space travel was still incredibly dangerous. In January 1986, the space shuttle *Challenger* broke up just after launch, killing everyone on board, including a school teacher who would have been one of the first civilians to go into space. It was another tragedy for NASA, and it resulted in them putting the space shuttle programme on hold for two years. A month after the disaster though, Mir, the first long-term, consistently inhabited space station, was put into space by the Soviets. Between 1986 and 1996, it was added to, like a LEGO model in orbit, and it became a place for cosmonauts to experience long periods in space

– hundreds of days at a time. Mir was visited by many international astronauts, as well as cosmonauts, and paved the way for co-operation between the USA and the former Soviet Union's space programmes, as astronauts flew in American space shuttles to the Russian space station.

Also in 1986, Katherine Johnson decided to retire from the job she loved at NASA. She had been working there for twenty-eight years, through the incredible changes of the twentieth century. From the days when she had been told "girls don't go to the research meetings", she had gone on to have her name on twenty-six scientific papers. Her work was recognized by her peers on several occasions throughout the 1980s with the NASA Langley Research Center Special Achievement award. But the end of her career at NASA did not mark the end of her importance.

Discovering Katherine Johnson

Katherine Johnson always believed that she should work to inspire and support others. She continued to be active within Alpha Kappa Alpha, and through her church. She volunteered, tutoring children in maths and talking to schoolchildren about her career. She told them to follow their passion, and to work as if someone was watching them: to do their best, all the time and every time. By this time, she had grandchildren and great-grandchildren of her own, and as they grew older, she preferred them to be able to work out maths problems in their heads before using a computer to solve them. She believed that being able to do 'mental maths' was an important skill to learn, a valuable workout for the brain.

In addition, Katherine found herself becoming more and more known for the work she had done and as a role model for the part she had played in NASA's space programme throughout her working life. She was honoured by a number of universities who awarded her honorary doctorates in recognition of her work, acknowledging that she had been conducting research at the highest level. Then, in 2015, she was awarded the Presidential Medal of Freedom by President Obama. It was the highest award that an American civilian can be awarded from their country.

In 2016, Margot Lee Shetterly published a book about the black American women who had worked at NASA. *Hidden Figures* became enormously successful and a film was made, bringing Katherine's story to more and more people. Katherine, when she was interviewed for the book, requested that it be not only about her but about all the women who worked there. She was modest, but not only that – she was a team player who had great perspective on what she had achieved, and wanted the truth to be told. She made it clear that there were many black, American heroines at NASA: she supported others just as she had been supported by others to reach the heights she had.

Then in 2017, NASA announced that their new, state-of-the-art building for research into computing would be named the Katherine G. Johnson Computational Research Facility.

Katherine's response to this news was typical of someone who had always maintained a strong

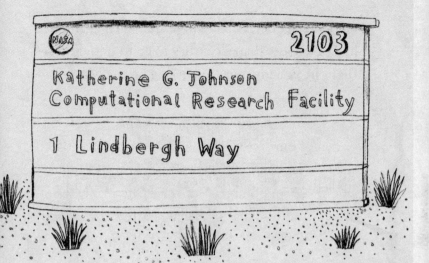

sense of perspective. "You want my honest answer? I think they're crazy," she said firmly. "Little did I think it would go this far!"

Looking back over a life that spanned a century and lived through segregation, spent working for joy not for personal recognition, it is easy to see why someone with Katherine's common sense would consider having a building named after her 'crazy'. The sheer enormity of the change that had happened in her life, from enduring segregated schools to having one of the most advanced research facilities in the world named after her, is incredible. But then again, it had taken less than a century to go from the first flight in an aeroplane, to landing on the Moon.

YOU HAVE TO BELIEVE PROGRESS WILL BE MADE,

Katherine was once quoted to have said in an interview. In her lifetime, it certainly had been made, and she has been one of the people who made it happen. She inspired so many others by setting an example of a confident, tough and intelligent woman working in science. She also set an invaluable precedent, by being a black American woman working at the cutting edge of technology within NASA, the organization that many saw as defining American achievement and glory.

In 1992, one of the people she indirectly inspired by making the Moon landings possible, Mae Jemison, finally got her dream: she became the first black American woman to travel into space on the space shuttle *Endeavour*. Perhaps it would finally become normal to choose the best person for the job, without prejudice.

Space for Everyone

The world of space exploration that Mae Jemison entered in 1992 was very different from the Moon-obsessed NASA that Katherine Johnson had been part of. In the 1990s, after the Soviet Union had dissolved, international cooperation was developing, and Russians and Americans were partners on space missions, a level of progress that would have been as unbelievable to anyone who had worked at NASA through the 1950s and '60s, as Katherine thought it was to have a computational research facility named after her. No one could have imagined, when they were looking up at Sputnik floating across the sky, that one day an American space shuttle would be flying up to a Russian space station, the two countries co-operating rather than competing.

But that was what was happening, and it was great for science. By combining what they had learned about space travel, countries could work together much more efficiently. How long could humans stay in space? Could food be grown in space? What did they have do to stay healthy up there? If people were ever going to live in space, these were the kind of questions that needed to be answered. By the end of the 1990s, work was well underway on the International Space Station that would replace Mir. The space shuttles had been designed for this, as 'space lorries' to help humans build structures and craft in orbit, and they were successfully carrying out their work in a new international way that had dreams even greater than the Moon.

One of the first telescopes in space was

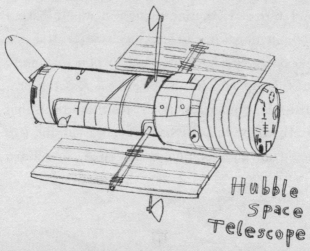

Hubble Space Telescope

the Hubble Space Telescope, which was put into orbit in 1990. In all, four observatories are currently in orbit. Looking out, without the interference of Earth's atmosphere to fog up the lenses, the pictures that Hubble and other telescopes sent back were incredible. Hubble proved the existence of black holes, which had previously been only a theory, and sent back information that helped scientists find out more about the way stars were born and died.

In 1996, NASA launched Pathfinder, carrying Sojourner, a rover that could explore the surface of Mars and send back images. It was an enormous success: Sojourner lasted longer than anyone had expected, and sent back hundreds of pictures of the red planet. In the same decade, the Cassini probe set off for Saturn, taking seven years to reach the planet, where it investigated the rings and sent down a probe to Titan, one of Saturn's largest moons, to sample the atmosphere. The search for water on planets and moons in the Solar System became an important focus for the probes that were being sent out: where there was water, there could be – or, once upon a time might have been

– life. "Follow the water" was NASA's new motto. A succession of missions and rovers revealed that there had once been water on Mars, meaning that the planet could once have supported life, even if that life was only tiny microorganisms.

In 2005, the Cassini probe found evidence of water on Enceladus, a moon of Saturn's. As further probes explored the Solar System, it seemed as if water – and possibly, life – was in more places than anyone had expected. To find life on other planets would be the next great first of space exploration. An alien encounter might not just be a great event in the history of science, it might also be a moment like seeing the first Earthrise that would give the human race a fresh way of seeing itself. But like all the great events in space exploration, such a moment would have begun with many, many first steps. When the probes left Earth and swung around the planets, using their roots in decades-old research, with gravity to propel them forward, they moved according to the same mathematical calculations that Katherine Johnson had done so many years ago to put the first American into space. If we ever find life outside Earth, we will be able to trace the beginning of that journey back, in part, to Katherine Johnson, the girl who asked questions – lots of questions.

A Team on Planet Earth

One of the benefits of filming the expeditions to the Moon is that much of that old footage is available to watch now, on the internet – a window into the incredible achievements of the past. Today, you can watch the *Apollo 11* Moon landing as soon as you close this book, and imagine how marvellous and incredible it must have been to see the adventure unfolding before your eyes for the first time. Some things stand out though, with the distance of time – most of all, how hard it is, not just to get to the Moon, but to be on the Moon at all. The astronauts lumber in their heavy, thick-fingered spacesuits, enormous boxes on their backs, slow and clown-like in the weak gravity of the Moon. Watching, it strikes the viewer now that the Moon is so hard to cling to, so hard to get to. It is so hard to leave Earth. Perhaps, in some sense, we always take Earth with us wherever we go? The astronauts fumble with the flag, spreading it out carefully, but the viewer notices at once that there is no wind on the Moon. A country's flag is so human, so Earth-bound. To get it to stay up, flying as if it were on Earth, the astronauts had to install a special rod, for the flag to hang down from. The flag is still up there, waiting for someone to see it. Of course, the most important audience was here on Earth.

In their visits to the Moon, humans left behind many things apart from the flag – from spacecraft parts to moon buggies, rubbish to bags of urine! Footprints remain untouched in the still atmosphere. But other things were left behind to act as messages. Some were messages to people on Earth, like the American flag. Astronaut Eugene Cernan, the last man to walk on the Moon, left his daughter's initials written in the dust on the Moon. Others were like messages in a bottle, to anyone else who might be out there, somewhere unimaginably distant in time and space.

Apollo 11 left a plaque inscribed with the event and the date, along with the words, "We came in peace for all mankind". A plaque and a small statue were also left by astronauts on *Apollo 15*, to honour the memory of astronauts and cosmonauts who had died in the course of getting to the Moon. If a new message were ever to be taken to the Moon, Katherine Johnson's family saying: "You are as good as, but no better than, anyone else," might be a good motto to help all humans remember that they are part of a team on planet Earth – and that some things, like prejudice, should be left behind in the past, for ever.

HOW SHOULD WE LIVE IN SPACE?

Can you design your own space station of the future? What rules should astronauts follow when they are up there? What sort of spaces will they need to eat and work and relax in? How will they feed themselves? You could draw a picture or make a model. Watch the broadcasts from the International Space Station to inspire you! https://www.nasa.gov/multimedia/nasatv/iss_ustream.html

YOUR FUTURE IN SPACE!

If Katherine Johnson were starting out today, she would find that there are plenty of exciting ways in which her career could develop. Instead of sending men to the Moon, scientists want to find out more about planets that humans could live on one day. For missions to other planets and solar systems, mathematicians like Katherine will have to calculate trajectories, taking into account the effects of the different gravitational forces on the spacecraft. Scientists also want to find out how to travel in the air and in space without damaging the environment. Nowadays, we know that we have to look after our own home planet first and foremost, and that we can't just take our environmentally destructive ways with us to other planets.

Today, many countries have space programmes, and private companies like SpaceX are also making serious attempts to get to the

Moon and to Mars. That means there are even more opportunities for exciting jobs in space exploration. If you want to follow in Katherine Johnson's footsteps, and work in aeronautics and space flight research, here are just some of the possible ways in which you could do that.

Can I Build Better Planes?

NASA and many other organizations across the world are eager to find more efficient and environmentally friendly ways of flying. As an aerospace scientist or an aeronautical engineer, you might find yourself working on the "X" planes – piloted, experimental aircraft that are designed to find ways in which new technology and better design can make air travel faster, quieter and better for the environment. One of the big problems for passenger aircraft, like Concorde, was the loud "sonic boom" that was created when planes broke the sound barrier. As a result, planes are not allowed to travel faster than the speed of sound when passing over land, only when they are over the sea. Researchers are now looking into ways of making that sonic boom much quieter – they're calling it a "sonic thump". They are also trying to design and build planes that will run on batteries – which will make air travel more environmentally friendly, as well as solar-powered planes. When the first aeroplanes were developed, engineers didn't realize the impact they would have on the environment. But, as an aerospace scientist of the future, making air travel cleaner should be top of your list of priorities!

Space scientists, too, now know that they need to be more mindful of the environment. Clearing up space debris is something that scientists now take very seriously. Most space debris is made up of bits of rock – asteroids and meteors that are "left over" from the formation of planets. But some of it is man-made. Bits and pieces from previous missions were left up in orbit around the Earth. These range from things like gloves, toothbrushes and cameras lost by astronauts on space walks, to whole booster rockets and dead satellites. The Vanguard 1 satellite that the USA launched in the 1950s is still up in orbit, and is expected to stay up there for 240 years, although it is no longer in use. These pieces of debris are now whizzing around Earth at thousands of miles an hour, and although space is big, there are over 17,000 large artificial objects up in orbit. There are over 170 million much smaller objects up there too – but even these tiny objects can cause real damage to any space station, satellite or spacecraft that they might hit. And the debris is bumping into other bits of debris too – breaking into smaller and smaller pieces as it does so, until anyone flying into space has to go through a hailstorm of dangerous rubbish.

As a space scientist or engineer of the future you might research and develop ways of "litter-picking" that fast-flying space rubbish, working with the most up-to-date technology to protect the planet. Current ideas for clearing up the dangerous mess orbiting the Earth include a remote-controlled space vehicle that goes out and catches debris and takes it back to a central station, a powerful laser "broom" that would break down the bits so they fall out of orbit and burn up in the atmosphere, and a harpoon that can shoot out and pull the debris back to safety. What other solutions might there be? Perhaps you can think of one!

Whichever solution they decide on, space scientists have to think hard both about how they clear up the mess left behind by the initial Space Race, and about how they design new spacecraft and satellites so they don't leave the same mess behind in the future. Dealing with space debris might also lead to new ways of defending the Earth against dangerous meteors – like the one that led to the extinction of the dinosaurs.

What Computers Would I Use As a Space Scientist?

While she was working at NASA, Katherine Johnson saw the incredible development of computers, from huge, room-filling machines to ones that flew men to the Moon, and later, to computers small enough to sit on a desk. Since then, computers have become smaller and smaller and faster and faster. In the future, space scientists may develop new systems of computing – such as quantum computers that use things called qubits to carry information, or DNA computers that use the structure of DNA to carry information – to conduct calculations far faster than today's computers. In fact, the computing technology to get people and robots to faraway planets is already in existence. The real barrier to deep space exploration isn't the technology, but the distances involved. It takes months just to fly to our nearest planet, Mars, and years to fly to the outskirts of the Solar System. It could take hundreds or even thousands of years to travel to other solar systems, and far longer than that to travel to other galaxies.

Scientists have begun exploring amazing and extraordinary ideas at the far frontiers of space travel. Those might not become possible for hundreds or thousands of years, or they might never become possible, but the work of imagining them has already begun. Space scientists know that one reason to look outside Earth and the Solar System is that humans, so far, have only one home. If something threatens the existence of our planet, we should be ready to move on.

Could I Go into Space?

Yes! Astronauts still fly up on space shuttles to work at and live in the International Space Station. They perform maintenance work on the station and carry out scientific experiments that can only be done in space or in low gravity environments. Some of these experiments aim to find out how humans might be affected by travelling to Mars, or to develop ways of making future manned missions to the Moon or Mars possible. Other experiments aim to find out more about Earth, for example, to try to understand weather patterns or how certain dangerous fluids that are used in machinery on Earth behave. You can watch live broadcasts from the International Space Station and follow NASA's blog to see what life as an astronaut is like.

However, you don't have to be an astronaut to explore space. Scientists on Earth have sent unmanned spacecraft, called probes, to the most distant planets in our Solar System and beyond. Probes have been sent to all major the planets in our Solar System, and to some of their moons, to take photographs and, where possible, to land and explore. The probes are controlled remotely from Earth. They have sent back detailed pictures from the surface of Mars, shown us that a moon of Jupiter may have liquid water on it, and photographed the rings of Saturn. The probes travelled on trajectories planned and plotted by mathematicians like Katherine Johnson, using the gravity of different planets, moons and the Sun, to pull them towards their destination.

Some of today's space scientists design, build

and work with telescopes that, like Hubble, are floating in outer space and sending images back to Earth. Space telescopes are just what they sound like: telescopes that are in space! Telescopes on Earth have to look through the Earth's atmosphere, which makes the images they can show quite blurry. That is why they are often on mountaintops, where the air is thinner. Telescopes in space don't have the atmosphere blocking their way, so they can send back much clearer images. Hubble is one of these space telescopes.

Using telescopes to look deeper and deeper into space is a very important part of understanding the Universe. Images from the newest space telescopes show us what the Universe looked like in its very early days. Telescopes help scientists answer questions like: what happens when two galaxies merge? How did stars and planets form in the first place, and what will happen to them after they die?

Could I Meet an Alien?

Possibly. As far as we know, Earth is the only planet to have life on it. But there are over 30 billion planets in our galaxy alone, and over 100 billion in the part of the Universe that we know about – and that is a mere fraction of the whole Universe! Given those facts, it seems highly unlikely that of all the hundreds and thousands of billions of planets out there just ONE has life. It seems more likely that if we look far enough and hard enough into space, we will find life of some kind.

Scientists nowadays can observe planets far outside our Solar System; planets that humans will probably never be able to visit because it takes so long to get there. These planets are called exoplanets, and one reason for looking for them is to search for alien life. Scientists work like detectives, putting evidence together to discover the probability that a planet might have, or might once have had, life on it. Something that strongly suggests a planet might be able to have life on it is whether it is in the "Goldilocks zone" of its star.

Planets that are too close to the star are too hot for life to survive, and planets that are too far away are too cold. Planet Earth is in this "just right" zone. That's why it is named after the little girl from the fairy tale *Goldilocks and the Three Bears*!

If scientists do discover life, it might only be single-celled organisms, but that's how all life on this planet started! It might also be life that is so different to the life on our planet that we don't immediately recognize it as life. By investigating extreme environments on Earth, such as vents at the bottom of the ocean and highly acidic environments, scientists have become aware that organisms can live in seemingly impossible places, with no oxygen or light or an obvious food source. Would we know an alien if we met it? Or might we not even recognize each other as living things?

Is There Life on Mars?

Mars is our closest planet, and the one that science fiction writers have always loved to make up stories about. There are almost certainly no little green men on Mars (if there are, they're hiding very well!) but Mars is of serious interest to space scientists. There is some evidence that life may have been possible at one time on Mars, and it may even be possible for humans to colonize it one day.

In 2020, several organizations will be sending unmanned missions to Mars. ExoMars, an international mission, will look for evidence of life. The United Arab Emirates will send Mars Hope, the first mission to be sent by a Muslim-majority country. The red planet may soon be dotted with flags!

Can I Walk on the Moon?

Why not? Just because humans haven't been back to the Moon since 1972, it doesn't mean that they will never go there again. In 2019, the unmanned Chinese spacecraft, *Chang'e 4*, landed on the far side of the Moon: the first spacecraft to ever touch the side of the Moon we never see from Earth. China has plans to land people on the Moon in the 2030s, and to possibly establish a base there. One of China's current experiments is to try and grow plants on the Moon in a small biosphere, using silk worms to produce carbon dioxide for the potato plants. The experiment will tell scientists more about how photosynthesis might work on the Moon, and may show them how future visitors to the Moon could feed themselves. India and the European Union also have active space programmes that recruit astronauts. Nowadays, private companies like SpaceX and Virgin are also building rockets and finding ways of travelling into space. If you don't want to go as far as the Moon, you can go for a short break in space. Private companies plan to offer expensive "space holidays". These trips would not last a very long time and would only go into low Earth orbit – but daring travellers would get to see Earth from space for themselves.

When Katherine Johnson was born in 1918, aeroplanes were built of wood and cloth, the world was ripped apart by war, black and white people in the USA were not allowed to marry or even share a bathroom, and American women didn't have the right to vote.

By 2018, when Katherine Johnson celebrated her hundredth birthday, men had walked on the Moon, America had elected its first black President, and astronauts of all colours and genders, from all over the world, were flying in space shuttles up to the space station orbiting Earth where they lived together for months at a time.

We can look back over the incredible century of her life and feel that because of the energy, intelligence and dedication of people like her, progress – despite all the barriers – has been made. In the future, perhaps the energy, intelligence and dedication of people like YOU will lead to even more progress!

PLAYLIST

THE WATCHERS

David Bowie, 'Space Oddity'

'Space Oddity' was released in 1969, the same year that *Apollo 11* put the first men on the Moon. It wasn't a big hit at first, but soon became perhaps the most famous space song of all.

AS GOOD AS, BUT NO BETTER THAN, ANYONE ELSE

Mavis Staples, 'We Shall Not Be Moved'

The civil rights movement was rich in songs of protest – this is one of the most famous.

WORK IS A JOY

Count Basie, 'Flying Home'

The lyrics of this jazz standard captured the excitement of early commercial air travel – with passengers sitting in the front being served champagne!

MASSIVE RESISTANCE

John Coltrane, 'Alabama'

Many powerful songs were written as a response to racist acts of violence that happened in the segregation era. *Alabama* was composed by legendary jazz musician John Coltrane, in response to the Ku Klux Klan's 1963 bombing of a church in Birmingham, Alabama, which killed four young Black American girls.

GETTING INTO SPACE

Public Service Broadcasting, 'Gagarin'

This track wasn't recorded until 2015, but it is part of a whole album that sampled real speeches, broadcasts and space noise from the Space Race.

GET THE GIRL TO CHECK

Bob Dylan, 'The Times They Are a-Changin''

The title summed it up: things were changing whether people liked it or not.

THREE DISASTERS

Mahalia Jackson, 'Precious Lord, Take My Hand'
The famous singer was a friend of Martin Luther King Jr and sang this hymn at his funeral.

THE MOON WILL BE THERE

The Inspiral Carpets, 'Saturn V'
This British band captured how uplifting it was to see the rocket Saturn V blasting off to the Moon!

LEGACY

Janelle Monae, 'Sally Ride'
Janelle Monae's tribute to the first American female astronaut.

YOUR FUTURE IN SPACE

....

Moby, 'Made of Stars'

The elements that make up all human life were created in the heart of stars!

TIMELINE OF KATHERINE JOHNSON'S LIFE

1918: Born in West Virginia.

1928: Begins high school.

1937: Graduates from West Virginia State College (now West Virginia State University) with degrees in maths and French.

1939: Marries James Francis Goble.

1953: Begins working at the National Advisory Committee for Aeronautics (NACA).

1956: James Francis Goble dies.

1957: Soviet Union launches Sputnik 1.

1958: NACA becomes the National Aeronautics and Space Administration (NASA), and Katherine's work changes to focus on the mathematics of space flight.

1960: Co-authors "Determination of Azimuth Angle at Burnout for Placing a Satellite Over a Selected Earth Position" with engineer Ted Skopinski.

1961: Calculates the trajectory for Alan Shepard's spacecraft, the first American in space.

1962: Calculates the flight path for John Glenn on his request, checking the electronic computer's calculations are correct.

1969: Works on the first lunar landing, and calculates the equations needed for the lunar rendezvous.

1986: Retires from NASA.

2015: Presented with the Presidential Medal of Freedom.

2017: NASA, Langley's Katherine Johnson Computational Research Facility officially opens.

TIMELINE OF
BLACK AMERICAN HISTORY

1865: Slavery abolished.

1870s: Many states introduce laws enforcing racial segregation.

1895: Author and sociologist William Du Bois is the first black American to be awarded a PhD, by Harvard University.

1896: The US Supreme Court rules in the case of Plessy vs Ferguson that it is legal to segregate on the basis of race.

1910: The National Association for the Advancement of Colored People (NAACP) is formed. This association fights to get black Americans the rights they are entitled to.

1931: Nine black American boys are arrested after being falsely accused of a crime. They are eventually sentenced to death. The racist trial of the "Scottsboro boys" is one of the most famous examples of the many unjust ways in which black Americans are treated across the USA at this time.

1951: Students at Robert Russa Moton High school (where Dorothy Vaughan had also worked) walk out in protest at the poor conditions in their segregated school.

1954: School segregation is outlawed following the case of Brown vs Board of Education. The US Supreme Court rules that, "Separate educational facilities are inherently unequal." However, many states refuse to stop segregation.

1955: Emmett Till, a fourteen-year-old boy is brutally murdered by a gang of white men who accuse him of offending a white woman. The murder leads to widespread disgust and anger, and encourages even more people to fight racism. In separate incidents, Claudette Colvin and Rosa Parks refuse to give up their seats on buses to a white person. Both were arrested, which led to the Montgomery Bus Boycott.

1958–1959: Senator Harry Byrd's policy of "massive resistance" means that he shuts the schools to white children as well as black children, rather than allow them to go to the same school.

1959: Mildred and Richard Loving, a couple that had married despite the fact that Mildred was black and Richard was white, are sentenced to a year in prison in Virginia, where interacial marriage is still illegal. The case goes to court and results in the laws against interracial marriage being overturned in 1967.

1960: Six-year-old Ruby Bridges receives death threats and has to have police protection when she becomes the first black child to start at a previously all-white school.

1964: Public segregation is outlawed. The Civil

Rights Act is passed. John Lennon announces that The Beatles will not play to a segregated audience in Jacksonville, Florida.

1968: Martin Luther King Jr is assassinated.

TIMELINE OF AVIATION

1903: The Wright brothers make the first successful aeroplane flight at Kitty Hawk, North Carolina.

1914–1918: During World War I, aeroplanes are mostly used for observation, though some are fitted with guns.

1921: Bessie Coleman becomes the first black American to gain a pilot's licence.

1927: Charles Lindbergh becomes the first person to fly nonstop across the Atlantic Ocean.

1930: The jet engine is invented by Frank Whittle, a British engineer – although it is only tested on the ground.

1932: Amelia Earhart becomes the first woman to fly solo across the Atlantic ocean.

1947: Test pilot Chuck Yeager breaks the sound barrier.

1952: First commercial jet flight, with paying passengers, is made in the British de Havilland Comet plane. Commercial flights quickly become popular, and letters and parcels can be delivered faster by airmail.

1953: Jackie Cochran becomes the first woman to break the sound barrier.

1956: Perry H. Young Jr becomes the first commercially employed black American helicopter pilot.

1958: Mohawk Airlines hires the first black American stewardess, Ruth Carol Taylor.

1963: Marlon D. Green wins a lawsuit against Continental Airlines to allow him to become a commercially employed American pilot, despite his race.

1964: American Airlines hires David Harris as the first black American pilot for a major commercial passenger airline.

1976: Concorde becomes the first supersonic passenger jet.

1986: The experimental aircraft, Voyager,

makes the first nonstop flight around the world.

2005: Steve Fossett makes the first nonstop flight around the world.

2016: The first flight powered by renewable energy (solar power) around the world is made, by Solar Impulse 2.

A SHORT HISTORY OF COMPUTING

The first computers were human beings like Katherine – they computed, or calculated, equations in their heads. Later, they did these sums with the help of mechanical desk calculators, which were about the size of desktop computers today. In 1947, NACA bought an "electronic calculator" from Bell Telephone Laboratories. It helped them to see how planes behaved at transonic speeds, as these behaviours were particularly complex to calculate. In the 1950s, NACA bought its first IBM computers. Katherine Johnson had to learn to program these machines.

Part of the computer that went to the Moon was assembled by women who worked at a weaving factory. Memory in the computer was nicknamed LOL memory – Little Old Lady memory! Computers in the 1960s were still huge and expensive. They were only owned by governments and big organizations. Few people thought that ordinary households would want computers. In the 1980s and 1990s, computers became smaller and cheaper – now everyone wanted one. Then the arrival of the internet in the 1990s made computers even more exciting. Today, the computer in a mobile phone is more powerful than the one used to send people to the Moon!

FURTHER READING

Books
Hidden Figures by Margot Lee Shetterly

Websites
NASA blog:
www.nasa.gov/mission_pages/station/research/news/
SSSH_18feb19

Interviews with Katherine Johnson
www.makers.com/profiles/591f267c6c3f646439558630
www.nasa.gov/audience/forstudents/k-4/stories/first-person-on-
moon.html
www.history.nasa.gov/ap11ann/apollo11_log/log.htm

GLOSSARY

Aerodynamics: having a shape which moves through the air quickly

Aeronautics: the science or practice of building or operating an aircraft

Atomic: something relating to the energy that is released when atoms are split

Aviation: the flying of aircraft

Axis: an imaginary line that goes through the centre of something, often used for reference and to show the position of a point

Colour bar: a social system that stopped black people and people from other races from accessing the same rights and opportunities as white people

Command module: a detachable, controlled area of a spacecraft

Communism: a political, social and economic system where different social classes are removed; property and produce are owned by everyone and shared equally

Confederate States: another term for the Confederacy, which was a group of southern states in the American Civil War that fought to keep slavery

Constellation: a group of stars that form a pattern in the sky

Cosmonaut: a Russian astronaut

Eclipse: when something is partially or completely blocked by something else, usually the Sun by the Moon

Federal: relating to the US central government. Individual states in the United States make their own laws but the central (federal) government is responsible for particular areas like defence

Fortran: a computer programming language that is especially used for mathematical and scientific calculations

Geometry: an area of mathematics that deals with the properties and relationships of lines, curves, points, angles and shapes

Gravity: a force that that pulls any thing with mass to the centre of a large planetary body

Jettison: to throw or drop items like fuel and goods from a ship or aircraft

Lunar module: a small craft used for travelling between an orbiting spacecraft and the Moon's surface

Nuclear: relating to the energy that is released when the nucleus of an atom is split or combined with another

Newsreel: a short film of news reports that used to be shown in the cinemas in the past

Orbit: the curved path of an object moving around a larger object in space, for example, a spacecraft around the Moon

Postgraduate: a course or study that is done by someone who has already completed a first undergraduate degree at university

Precedent: an action or situation that has already happened that is used an example as to why something should happen again

Prejudice: an unreasonable opinion or dislike that is not based on reason or experience

Protocol: an official set of rules for acceptable behaviour at ceremonies or formal occasions

Retrorocket: a small rocket on a spacecraft that fires in the opposite direction of the flight to slow down the spacecraft or move it backwards

Revolution: an overthrow of the government or political system for a new one, often by force

Satellite: an orbiting device that is sent up to space to send and receive information

Segregation: the act of separating something or keeping different groups of people apart from one another

Specialism: an area of work or study that someone has a lot of knowledge about

Soviet Union: the group of Communist states that occupied part of Eastern Europe and Northern Asia; its capital was Moscow

Supremacy: the state of being superior or in a leading position over others

Surveillance: the careful observation of someone or something

Test pilot: a person who flies a new aircraft to test out its performance

Trajectory: the path that follows a moving object as it moves through the air

Union states: a group of (mostly) northern states led by the President of the USA that opposed the Confederate states in the American Civil War

Van Allen radiation belt: a broad zone of intense radiation far above the Earth's surface, made up of high-energy electrons and protons

INDEX